THE REPORT CARD

The Savvy Family's Guide to Chicago High Schools

LINDA A. THORNTON

REF LB 1607.52 .I5 T5 2003
Thornton, Linda A.
The Report card

CHICAGO PUBLIC LIBRARY
WEST ENGLEWOOD BRANCH
1745 W. 63rd STREET
CHICAGO, IL 60636

The Report Card: The Savvy Family's Guide to Chicago High Schools
© Copyright 2003 by Linda A. Thornton

International Standard Book Number: 1-929612-46-X
Library of Congress Catalog Number: 2003092471

All rights reserved. No part of this book may be reproduced in any form or by any electronic or mechanical means, including information storage and retrieval systems, without written permission from the author, except by reviewers who may quote brief passages in reviews.

PRINTED IN THE UNITED STATES OF AMERICA

Adams Press
Chicago, Illinois
www.adamspress.com

To Michael and Alexander:
The other two peas in my pod.

To my Mom and Dad:
My guiding lights.

TABLE OF CONTENTS

Introduction vi

Steps for High School Admission viii

HIGH SCHOOLS
Catholic..1
Independent 33
Public 45

Public High School Regions 123

The ABC's of High School Terminology 125

Index 135

How to 138
   Order this book
   Use this book as a fundraising tool
   Enhance fundraising efforts with a guest speaker
   Add a high school to the listing

INTRODUCTION

A UNIQUE ADMISSIONS PROCESS
The high school admissions process in the City of Chicago is unique. In suburban areas, students generally attend their local, neighborhood high school. Here in the city, however, students may choose from Catholic, independent, or public schools...and the choices continue from there. Will you, as a parent, pay $17,800 a year for your student to attend Lake Forest Academy, or will you have no tuition to pay if your student attends a public school? Will your student walk to school or commute daily to Loyola Academy in Wilmette? And once you have chosen a school, will that school accept your student? What are the admission policies and protocol? Which school's philosophy is best suited to your student? How do you go about making this very important decision?

DON'T WAIT UNTIL EIGHTH GRADE
By eighth grade, unsuspecting parents and students are in frenzy. Come September, families are inundated with too much information that must be processed in too short a time. Open house schedules fill weekday evenings and weekends—sometimes you have no choice, but to attend two in one day. Last year, families hoped to have all their questions answered at the Chicago Public Schools' High School Fair and were surprised to find more than thirty thousand others with the same idea! Shadow Day invitations come and go, and before you know it, it's November and time to make decisions about where to take placement exams.

MOM ON A MISSION
The entire process is stressful, competitive, and intimidating, and up until now, there has never been one source for information. I know because I was a "Mom on a mission." Once my son entered

middle school, I intended to seek out all the information I could solely for our family's needs, but as I spoke to more and more parents—all of whom were, like me, desperate for accurate information—I decided to research the entire process and share my findings with other families.

THE BOOK NO MIDDLE SCHOOL PARENT SHOULD BE WITHOUT
The Report Card: The Savvy Family's Guide to Chicago High Schools demystifies the complicated high school admission process. It lists more than one hundred schools by category (Catholic, independent, and public) and provides the reader with all the general information he or she needs to know about each individual school (there's even an area for you to jot down your own notes). The section entitled "The ABCs of High School Terminology" defines and explains more than forty common terms in an easy A–Z format. Finally, the timeline in "Steps for High School Admission" shares the best kept secret of all: how to spread the search process over the middle school years, eliminate stress, and enjoy an important family experience.

SIR FRANCIS BACON: "KNOWLEDGE IS POWER"
It is a known fact that there are more eager, qualified students than freshman openings at most Chicago-area high schools. Therefore, securing the competitive edge becomes the all important factor that will affect the next four years of your student's life and his or her ultimate success.
Arming yourself with all the information you require to make this very important decision will make your task much easier. I wish each of you the very best of luck.

LINDA A. THORNTON
THE REPORT CARD:
The Savvy Family's Guide to Chicago High Schools

STEPS FOR HIGH SCHOOL ADMISSION

The secret to a stress-free experience

Many families begin the high school selection process during the fall of their student's eighth grade year. This gives families only a couple of months to digest an abundance of information and make a decision, whether they have all their questions answered or not.

Spreading out the search process over a student's middle school years greatly lessens the stress factor and makes this very important project an enjoyable and exciting family experience.

6th Grade

1. Begin discussing school choices. Some points to consider:
   a. Catholic vs. independent vs. public
   b. Coed vs. single gender
   c. Location of school/daily commute
   d. School's size
   e. School's style
   f. Your student's personality
   g. Your student's scholastic ability
2. Send for brochures
3. Speak with high school students and their families

7th Grade

1. Attend high school fairs
2. Attend high school open houses
3. Speak with your current school's teachers and principal and obtain their input
4. Begin narrowing down your choices

8th Grade

1. Make your final selection of two or three high schools
2. Re-attend the open houses of your top choices
   a. Concentrate on things you may have missed the first time around
      1. Are the bathrooms graffiti free?
      2. What's featured in the display cases?
      3. How does the cafeteria look?
   b. Ask the students some questions
      1. What do they like most and least about the school?
      2. How they did they come to choose this particular school?
3. Students: sign up for a Shadow Day at your top choices
4. Parents: visit those schools on your own on a regular school day. Just a ten minute walk down the hall as classes change can give you much information
   a. Do you hear abusive language from the students?
   b. Are students moving briskly to their next class?
   c. Are teachers in evidence to herd students or are they conversing with them civilly?
5. Apply to your top choices (obtain application and/or placement exam date)
6. Follow up with your student's current school to make sure that requested information is sent to the high schools (transcripts, etc.) by the dates requested
7. Students: prepare for placement exams
8. Students: take the placement exams
   a. Depending on your choice of Catholic, independent or public schools, you may be taking up to three exams
   b. Remember to take the Catholic school placement exam at your *first* choice school
9. If accepted, notify the school of your decision immediately
10. If rejected by your first choice school, request that your test scores be sent on to your second choice

CATHOLIC HIGH SCHOOLS

Boys

Archbishop Quigley Preparatory Seminary 3
Brother Rice High School 4
Hales Franciscan High School 10
Leo High School 13
Mount Carmel High School 18
Notre Dame High School 20
St. Patrick High School 28
St. Rita of Cascia High School 29

Girls

Good Counsel High School 8
Josephinum High School 12
Maria High School 15
Mother McAuley High School 17
Notre Dame High School 19
Our Lady of Tepeyac High School 21
Regina Dominica High School 22
Resurrection High School 23
St. Scholastica Academy 30
Trinity High School 31
Woodlands Academy of the Sacred Heart 32

Coed

Cristo Rey Jesuit High School 5
De La Salle Institute 6
Fenwick High School 7

Gordon Tech High School 9
Holy Trinity High School 11
Loyola Academy 14
Marist High School 16
St. Benedict High School..24
St. Francis de Sales High School 25
St. Gregory High School 26
St. Ignatius College Prep. High School 27

Archbishop Quigley Preparatory Seminary
103 East Chestnut Street • Chicago, IL 60611
(312) 787-9343 • Fax: (312) 787-9167

Website:	www.quigley.org	Email:	info@quigley.org
Principal:	The Rev. Peter Sneig	Admissions:	Mr. Vincent Vera
# in School:	210	# Freshmen:	50–65
Class Size:	20	Student/Faculty Ratio:	6:1
Tuition:	$5,000/$5,300	Other Expenditures:	
			Books: $300
			Raffle Tickets: $200

Profile:
Est. 1905. Traditional, College prep. Historic 1917 Gothic style building near Magnificent Mile. AP and honors courses. Students must be open to the idea of joining the priesthood. Listed in *U.S. News and World Report's* "96 Outstanding American High Schools," January 1999.

Public Transportation:
1 block west of Water Tower. CTA el: Howard Red Line; bus: #145, #146, #151; Metra train.

Dress Code:
Shirt and tie, 3 days; Quigley polo or collar shirt, 2 days; dress slacks.

Admission Requirements:
Must be baptized and confirmed Roman Catholic (because of seminary status); application; placement exam; pastor and principal recommendations.

Scholarships:
Full, half, and $500 based on placement exam score, grades, student essay, pastor and principal recommendations.

Notes:

Catholic High Schools • Boys

Brother Rice High School
1001 South Pulaski Road • Chicago, IL 60655
(773) 779-3410 • Fax: (773) 779-5239

Website:	www.brrice.chi.il.us	Email:	jek@brrice.chi.il.us
Principal:	Mr. James P. Antos	Admissions:	Mr. John Konecki
# in School:	1200	# Freshmen:	340
Class Size:	10–35	Student/Teacher Ratio:	18:1
Tuition:	$5,050/$5,450	Other Expenditures:	
			Fundraising: $150

Profile:
Est. 1956. College prep. Rooted in the philosophy of Br. Edmund Ignatius Rice, founder of the Congregation of Christian Brothers. One of the largest technologically advanced libraries in the state. Programs for both gifted (Focus) and struggling students (Apex). Recognized as a Blue Ribbon School.

Public Transportation:
CTA bus: 99th, 100th Streets.

Dress Code:
Button-down shirt and tie (polo shirt in warm weather); khaki slacks; dress shoes.

Admission Requirements:
Placement exam.

Scholarships:
Based on placement exam.

Notes:

The Report Card

Catholic High Schools • Coed

Cristo Rey Jesuit High School
1852 West 22nd Place • Chicago, IL 60608
(773) 890-6800 • Fax: (773) 890-6801

Website:	www.cristorey.net	Email:	rsantiago@cristorey.net
Principal:	Ms. Patricia Garrity	Admissions:	Ms. Rosie Santiago
# in School:	400	# Freshmen:	125–135
Class Size:	26	Student/Faculty Ratio:	N/A
Tuition:	$2,200/$2,200	Other Expenditures:	None

Profile:
Originally founded for immigrant children in Pilsen/Little Village neighborhood. Promotes religious and cultural heritage. Dual language school with graduates literate both in English and Spanish. Unique corporate internship program (students earn up to 70 percent tuition by working at local businesses).

Public Transportation:
CTA el: Blue Line.

Dress Code:
Business wear.

Admission Requirements:
Placement exam; transcripts; interview; knowledge of Spanish language.

Scholarships:
N/A

Notes:

Catholic High Schools • Coed

De La Salle Institute
3455 South Wabash Avenue • Chicago, IL 60616
(312) 842-7355 • Fax: (312) 842-5640

Website:	www.dls.org	Email:	broganj@dls.org
Principal:	Mr. James Krygier	Admissions:	Mr. John Brogan
# in School:	870	# Freshmen:	270
Class Size:	25	Student/Faculty Ratio:	N/A
Tuition:	$5,350/$5,555	Other Expenditures:	
			Books: $300

Profile:
Est. 1889. College prep. Oldest Catholic high school in Chicago at original site. Rooted in tradition of St. John Baptist De La Salle: to educate all. Honors and assistance programs. Consolidation with Lourdes High School in 2002–03 school year to form two campuses providing single-gender education, an unprecedented concept in Catholic education. Recognized as a Blue Ribbon School.

Public Transportation:
CTA el: Red Line, Green Line.

Dress Code:
Black, navy or khaki slacks or skirt; white or light blue button-down blouse or oxford cloth shirt.

Admission Requirements:
Placement exam.

Scholarships:
Up to 20 percent of tuition, based on placement exam.

Notes:

The Report Card

Fenwick High School
505 West Washington Boulevard • Oak Park, IL 60302
(708) 386-0127 • Fax: (708) 386-3052

Website:	www.fenwickfriars.com	Email:	pvandewalle@fenwickfriars.com
Principal:	Dr. James J. Quaid	Admissions:	Mr. Patrick Van DeWalle
# in School:	1,142	# Freshmen:	300
Class Size:	17	Student/Faculty Ratio:	1:16
Tuition:	$7,000/$7,300	Other Expenditures:	
			Books: $400

Profile:
Est. 1929. College prep. Dominican tradition (religious and cultural heritage in a Christian atmosphere). Draws students from 27 suburbs. An exemplary U.S. Department of Education school design. Listed in *U.S. News and World Report's* "96 Oustanding American High Schools," January 1999. Recognized as a Blue Ribbon School.

Public Transportation:
Metra Train. Fenwick buses offer near north and south bus routes and bus to and from Metra Train Station at an extra cost.

Dress Code:
Boys: button-down shirt, dress slacks, dress shoes; girls: uniform skirt, blouse, or turtleneck, dress shoes.

Admission Requirements:
Placement exam.

Scholarships:
$1,500 per year for four years if placement exam in the 99th percentile.

Notes:

Catholic High Schools • Girls

Good Counsel High School
3900 West Peterson • Chicago, IL 60659
(773) 478-3655 • Fax: (773) 478-6029

Website:	www.goodcounselhs.org	Email:	muhrickgc@aol.com
Principal:	Ms. Megan Quaile	Admissions:	Ms. Mary Uhrick
# in School:	410	# Freshmen:	90
Class Size:	16–21	Student/Faculty Ratio:	17:1
Tuition:	$5,420/$5,720	Other Expenditures:	Books: $470

Profile:
Est. 1926. College prep. Racially and ethnically diverse. Serving the north side of Chicago. Liberal arts curriculum in a technology rich environment. This school may be closing at the end of the 2003 school year.

Public Transportation:
CTA bus: Pulaski/Peterson.

Dress Code:
Gray uniform, white top, sweater.

Admission Requirements:
Placement exam, transcripts, and attendance.

Scholarships:
Based on 98th and 99th percentile of placement exam.

Notes:

The Report Card

Gordon Technical High School

3633 North California Avenue • Chicago, IL 60618
(773) 539-3600 • Fax: (773) 539-9158

Website:	www.gordontech.org	Email:	admin@gordontech.org
Principal:	Dr. Jo Ann Rapp	Admissions:	Ms. Mary Ellen Nickels
# in School:	800	# Freshmen:	200
Class Size:	25	Student/Faculty Ratio:	17:1
Tuition:	$5,600/$5,925	Other Expenditures:	
			Registration: $300
			Fundraisers: volunteer or donate

Profile:
Est. 1952. College prep. Focus on technology and fine arts. One of largest libraries in the Chicago Catholic School system. State-of-the-art technology lab, first of its kind in any Chicago Archdiocese high school. Known for racial and ethnic diversity. Coed beginning 2002–03 school year (freshmen and sophomore transfers only).

Public Transportation:
CTA bus: Addison.

Dress Code:
Boys: dress slacks, Gordon Tech polo shirt; girls: black skirt, white blouse.

Admission Requirements:
Placement exam.

Scholarships:
$1,000 and $500, based on placement exam.

Notes:

Catholic High Schools • Boys

Hales Franciscan High School
4930 South Cottage Grove Avenue • Chicago, IL 60615
(773) 285-8400 • Fax: (773) 285-7025

Website:	www.halesfranciscan.org	Email:	cmoorehales@yahoo.com
Principal:	Ms. Avis Wright	Admissions:	Mr. Charlton Moore
# in School:	350	# Freshmen:	115
Class Size:	16	Student/Faculty Ratio:	15:1
Tuition:	$3,750/$3,900	Other Expenditures:	N/A

Profile:
Est. 1962. College prep. Mostly African-American student population. Small size allows for academic development, awareness and respect of cultural heritage. Recognized as a Blue Ribbon School.

Public Transportation:
CTA bus: Cottage Grove Avenue.

Dress Code:
Khaki slacks, white button-down shirt, tie, dress shoes.

Admission Requirements:
Placement exam, transcripts.

Scholarships:
100 percent of tuition and 50 percent of tuition, based on exam percentile.

Notes:

Catholic High Schools • Coed

Holy Trinity High School
1443 West Division Street • Chicago, IL 60622
(773) 278-4212 • Fax: (773) 278-0144

Website:	www.htathletics.org	Email:	mstratman@holytrinity-hs.org
Principal:	Ms. Charlene Szumilas	Admissions:	Ms. Melinda Stratman
# in School:	400	# Freshmen:	125
Class Size:	15–20	Student/Faculty Ratio:	11:1
Tuition:	$4,900/$5,200	Other Expenditures:	
			Books: $400
			Registration: $100
			Fundraising: $175

Profile:
College prep. Honors and AP courses. Corporate internships (summer). One-on-one mentoring and tutoring. Diverse student body. Bilingual (Spanish, English). Promotes Spanish culture and heritage. State-of-the-art computer labs.

Public Transportation:
CTA bus: Division Street.

Dress Code:
Solid color slacks or skirt (no jeans); Holy Trinity polo shirt, sweatshirt, or sweater.

Admission Requirements:
Placement exam, transcripts.

Scholarships:
Based on placement exam: at or above 85th percentile = $2,250 (if 3.5 GPA maintained).

Notes:

Catholic High Schools • Girls

Josephinum High School
1501 North Oakley Boulevard • Chicago, IL 60622
(773) 276-1261 • Fax: (773) 292-3963

Website:	www.josephinum.org	**Email:**	See website
Principal:	Sr. Donna Collins, RSCJ	**Admissions:**	Ms. Zulma Ortiz
# in School:	200	**# Freshmen:**	50
Class Size:	20	**Student/Faculty Ratio:**	N/A
Tuition:	$3,900/$4,100	**Other Expenditures:**	
			Books: $100
			Uniforms: $100

Profile:
Est. 1890. College prep. Affordable inner city high school serving young women of various ethnic and religious backgrounds. Small class size and personal attention.

Public Transportation:
CTA el: Blue Line.

Dress Code:
Blue skirt or slacks, white polo shirt.

Admission Requirements:
Placement exam, transcripts, discipline, attendance.

Scholarships:
Based on placement exam.

Notes:

Catholic High Schools • Boys

Leo High School
7901 South Sangamon Street • Chicago, IL 60620
(773) 224-9600 • Fax: (773) 224-3856

Website:	www.leohighschool.org	**Email:**	See website
Principal:	Mr. Peter W. Doyle	**Admissions:**	Mr. Jerry Tokars
# in School:	350	**# Freshmen:**	100
Class Size:	25	**Student/Faculty Ratio:**	N/A
Tuition:	$4,125/$4,125	**Other Expenditures:**	Books: $275

Profile:
College prep. Range of programs for urban minority students. Only school in Illinois to offer Learning Logic computer-based algebra program developed by the National Science Foundation. Sylvan Learning Center operates on campus. Career Path program works with local companies.

Public Transportation:
CTA bus: 79th Street.

Dress Code:
Dark slacks, white collar shirt, tie, no sneakers.

Admission Requirements:
Placement exam.

Scholarships:
Based on placement exam: 90th percentile = $1,000; 80th–90th percentile = $500.

Notes:

Catholic High Schools • Coed

Loyola Academy
1100 Laramie Avenue • Wilmette, IL 60091
(847) 256-1100 • Fax: (847) 853-4512

Website:	www.goramblers.org	Email:	lseitzinger@loy.org
Principal:	The Rev. Terence A. Baum, SJ	Admissions:	Mr. Les Seitzinger
# in School:	2,000	# Freshmen:	520–560
Class Size:	23	Student/Faculty Ratio:	17:1
Tuition:	$7,700/$8,150	Other Expenditures:	Books: $350–$500

Profile:
Est. 1909. College prep. Traditional, liberal arts education with strong spiritual side. One of the nation's most respected high schools.

Public Transportation:
CTA el: Purple Line; Metra train.

Dress Code:
Slacks (no jeans or skirts); shirt or blouse with collar.

Admission Requirements:
Placement exam, transcripts.

Scholarships:
N/A

Notes:

Catholic High Schools • Girls

Maria High School
6727 South California Avenue • Chicago, IL 60629
(773) 925-8686 • Fax: (773) 925-8885

Website:	www.mariahighschool.org	Email:	See website
Principal:	Ms. Kathleen King	Admissions:	Mr. Scott Weakley
# in School:	800	# Freshmen:	200
Class Size:	20	Student/Faculty Ratio:	N/A
Tuition:	$5,300/$5,400	Other Expenditures: Uniform: $125	

Profile:
Est. 1952. College prep. Flexible curriculum to meet needs of different academic levels. Honors and AP courses. Sylvan Learning Lab for developmental courses. Business internship programs.

Public Transportation:
CTA el: Orange Line; bus: California Avenue.

Dress Code:
Each class wears different uniform. Freshmen: gray slacks or skirt, white polo shirt.

Admission Requirements:
Placement exam, transcripts.

Scholarships:
Based on placement exam.

Notes:

The Report Card

Catholic High Schools • Coed

Marist High School
4200 West 115th Street, Chicago, IL 60655
(773) 881-5300; Fax: (773) 881-0595

Website:	www.marist.net	Email:	gene@marist.net
Principal:	Mr. Larry Tucker	Admissions:	Mr. Gene Nolan
# in School:	1,250	# Freshmen:	490
Class Size:	28	Student/Faculty Ratio:	16:1
Tuition:	$4,900/$5,300	Other Expenditures:	
			Books: $200
			Registration: $150

Profile:
Est. 1963. College prep. AP classes. Founded by the Marist Brothers. Fifty-five-acre campus. One of the top computer programs in Illinois. Recognized as a Blue Ribbon School.

Public Transportation:
CTA bus: 115th Street/Pulaski Avenue; Marist bus also available.

Dress Code:
Slacks, skirt, button-down blouse or shirt (Friday: Marist polo shirt).

Admission Requirements:
Placement exam, transcripts, teacher recommendations.

Scholarships:
Based on placement exam: $1,000–$1,250 annually.

Notes:

The Report Card

Catholic High Schools • Girls

Mother McAuley Liberal Arts High School
3737 West 99th Street • Chicago, IL 60655
(773) 881-6500 • Fax: (773) 881-6562

Website:	www.mothermcauley.org	Email:	cwhite@mothermcauley.org
Principal:	Sr. Rose Wiorek, RSM	Admissions:	Ms. Colleen White
# in School:	1,885	# Freshmen:	500
Class Size:	17	Student/Faculty Ratio:	17.5:1
Tuition:	5,200/$5,600	Other Expenditures:	
			Books: $450

Profile:
Est. 1846. College prep. Nationally recognized faith-based educational programs. Largest Catholic girls high school in the U.S. Recognized as a Blue Ribbon School.

Public Transportation:
CTA bus: Pulaski.

Dress Code:
Uniform (each level casts vote): skirt, white polo shirt with school emblem.

Admission Requirements:
Placement exam.

Scholarships:
Based on placement exam: 99th percentile = 50 percent of tuition. Also $1,000 leadership-based and $500 for students of alumnae.

Notes:

The Report Card

Catholic High Schools • Boys

Mount Carmel High School
6410 South Dante Avenue • Chicago, IL 60637
(773) 324-1020 • Fax: (773) 324-9235

Website:	www.mchs.org	**Email:**	mcurta@mhs.org
Principal:	The Rev. Carl J. Markelz	**Admissions:**	Mr. Mike Curta
# in School:	830	**# Freshmen:**	250
Class Size:	25–30	**Student/Faculty Ratio:**	N/A
Tuition:	$4,850/$5,150	**Other Expenditures:**	
			Books: $400
			Fundraising: $300
			Registration: Fee $150

Profile:
Est.1900. College prep. Honors and AP courses. Special developmental programs available. More state sports championships than any other high school in the Archdiocese. First private high school in Chicago to be honored by the U.S. Department of Education as an exemplary private school.

Public Transportation:
Metra train: 63rd Street. Mount Carmel bus also available at extra cost.

Dress Code:
Dress slacks, shirt with collar, no sneakers.

Admission Requirements:
Placement exam.

Scholarships:
Based on placement exam: 99th percentile = $1,500; 90th percentile = $500.

Notes:

Catholic High Schools • Girls

Notre Dame High School
3000 North Mango Avenue • Chicago, IL 60634
(773) 622-9494 • Fax: (773) 622-8511

Website:	www.ndhs4girls.org	Email:	kbooth@ndhs4girls.org
Principal:	Ms. Karen Brown	Admissions:	Ms. Karen Booth
# in School:	500	# Freshmen:	140
Class Size:	20	Student/Faculty Ratio:	18:1
Tuition:	$4,970/$5,420	Other Expenditures:	N/A

Profile:
Est.1938. College prep. Emphasis on technology (technology integrated curriculum). One of the first schools in the Archdiocese to be fully Internet wired. Recognized as a Blue Ribbon School.

Public Transportation:
CTA bus: Central, Diversey, Austin, Belmont.

Dress Code:
Skirt, polo shirt, sweater.

Admission Requirements:
Placement exam.

Scholarships:
Based on placement exam: up to $1,400.

Notes:

The Report Card

Catholic High Schools • Boys

Notre Dame High School
7655 West Dempster Street • Niles, IL 60714
(847) 965-2900 • Fax: (847) 965-2975

Website:	www.ndhsdons.org	Email:	lbontempo@ndhsdons.org
Principal:	Mr. Paul Maloney	Admissions:	Mr. Dennis Zelasko
# in School:	700	# Freshmen:	215
Class Size:	25	Student/Faculty Ratio:	N/A
Tuition:	$5,950/$6,300	Other Expenditures:	
			Books: $300
			Activities: $500

Profile:
College prep. Traditional atmosphere based on faith, scholarship, service. Gifted and learning assistance programs available.

Public Transportation:
CTA el: Blue Line/Haile/Higgins.

Dress Code:
Docker slacks, polo shirt (any color).

Admission Requirements:
Placement exam.

Scholarships:
Based on placement exam.

Notes:

Our Lady of Tepeyac High School

2228 South Whipple Street • Chicago, IL 60623
(773) 522-0023 • Fax: (773) 522-0508

Website: www.tepeyachighschool.org	**Email:** tepayac@aol.com
Principal: Sr. Kathryn Wojcik, CR	**Admissions:** Ms. Isabel Del Real
# in School: 300	**# Freshmen:** 75
Class Size: 25	**Student/Faculty Ratio:** 25:1
Tuition: $2,700/$2,900	**Other Expenditures:**
	Books: $150
	Registration: $100
	Uniform: $100

Profile:
Est. 1928. College prep. Serving mostly Latin- and African-American students in Pilsen/Little Village community.

Public Transportation:
CTA el: Blue Line; bus: Cermac, 26th Street.

Dress Code:
Skirt (each class wears different color); white blouse with collar.

Admission Requirements:
Placement exam.

Scholarships:
N/A

Notes:

Catholic High Schools • Girls

Regina Dominican High School
701 Locust Road • Wilmette, IL 60091
(847) 256-7660 • Fax: (847) 256-3726

Website:	www.rdhs.org	Email:	euran@rdhs.org
Principal:	Nancy McCabe, Ph.D.	Admissions:	Ms. Erica Meghan
# in School:	450	# Freshmen:	130
Class Size:	15	Student/Faculty Ratio:	15:1
Tuition:	$7,200/$7,500	Other Expenditures:	
			Labs: (depends on class)

Profile:
Est. 1958. College prep. Dedicated to academic excellence and Christian values. Largest Catholic girls' athletic program in the state. Recognized as a Blue Ribbon School.

Public Transportation:
CTA el: Purple Line then Pace bus.

Dress Code:
Plaid skirt, white polo shirt. After sophomore year, girls vote for choice of plaid; freshmen wear second choice.

Admission Requirements:
Placement exam.

Scholarships:
Based on placement exam.

Notes:

Resurrection High School
7500 West Talcott • Chicago, IL 60631
(773) 775-6616 • Fax: (773) 775-0611

Website:	www.reshs.org	Email:	website@reshc.org
Principal:	Ms. Jo Marie Yonkus	Admissions:	Ms. Laura Tully
# in School:	950	# Freshmen:	260
Class Size:	10–25	Student/Faculty Ratio:	13:1
Tuition:	$5,000/$5,200	Other Expenditures:	
			Books: $375
			Uniforms: $200

Profile:
Est. 1912. College prep. Eleven million-dollar construction upgrade. Listed in *U.S. News and World Report's* "96 Oustanding American High Schools," January, 1999. Received 2002 Presidential award; named National Service Learning Leader School for its students' nonmandatory 41,000 hours of community service.

Public Transportation:
CTA el: Blue Line then Pace bus; Resurrection bus also available at extra cost.

Dress Code:
Students vote for uniform style.

Admission Requirements:
Placement exam.

Scholarships:
Based on placement exam: $500, $1,000.

Notes:

Catholic High Schools • Coed

St. Benedict High School
3900 North Leavitt • Chicago, IL 60018
(773) 539-0066 • Fax: (773) 539-3397

Website:	www.stbenedict.com	Email:	dpalumbo@stbenedict.com
Principal:	Ms. Mary Kay Nickels	Admissions:	Ms. Diane Palumbo
# in School:	465	# Freshmen:	100
Class Size:	17–20	Student/Faculty Ratio:	18:1
Tuition:	$5,220/$5,675	Other Expenditures:	
			Books: $400
			Registration: $125

Profile:
Est. 1950. College prep. Recent endowment responsible for new, three-story building addition. One of only three high schools in the Archdiocese on the same street with an elementary school. Consistently able to maintain one of the lowest annual tuitions among Catholic high schools.

Public Transportation:
CTA el: Ravenswood Brown Line; bus: Irving Park, Damen, Western, Addison.

Dress Code:
Boys: Blue or black slacks, white collar shirt; girls: plaid skort.

Admission Requirements:
Placement exam.

Scholarships:
Based on placement exam: $500–$2,000.

Notes:

Catholic High Schools • Coed

St. Francis de Sales High School
10155 South Ewing Avenue • Chicago, IL 60617
(773) 731-7272 • Fax: (773) 731-7888

Website:	www.stfrancisdesaleshs.net	**Email:**	sfdsl@aol.com
Principal:	Mr. Richard Hawkins	**Admissions:**	Mr. Jeff Fiedler
# in School:	375	**# Freshmen:**	125
Class Size:	20–25	**Student/Faculty Ratio:**	14:1
Tuition:	$4,800/$5,100	**Other Expenditures:**	
			Uniforms: $150
			Books: $250

Profile: College prep. Richly diverse student population. Committed to Christian education for more than 100 years.

Public Transportation:
CTA bus: 102nd Street/Ewing Avenue.

Dress Code:
Black, navy, or khaki slacks or skirt; school polo shirt; school sweater.

Admission Requirements:
Placement exam.

Scholarships:
Based on placement exam results.

Notes:

Catholic High Schools • Coed

St. Gregory High School
1677 West Bryn Mawr Avenue • Chicago, IL 60660
(773) 907-2100 • Fax: (773) 907-2120

Website:	www.stgregory.org	Email:	tom@stgregory.org
Principal:	Mr. Thomas Bearden	Admissions:	Ms. Joan Riise
	Dr. Thomas Gattuso		
# in School:	305	# Freshmen:	75
Class Size:	20–25	Student/Faculty Ratio:	30:1
Tuition:	4,880/$5,000	Other Expenditures:	
			Books: $300

Profile:
Est. 1937. College and career prep. Small student population and individual curricula to assist students with wide range of abilities. Secure and caring environment.

Public Transportation:
CTA el: Red and Brown Lines; bus: Damen.

Dress Code:
Dress slacks, St. Gregory polo shirt.

Admission Requirements:
Placement exam.

Scholarships:
N/A

Notes:

Catholic High Schools • Coed

St. Ignatius College Prep High School
1076 West Roosevelt Road • Chicago, IL 60608
(312) 421-5900 • Fax: (312) 421-7124

Website:	www.ignatius.org	Email:	claire.larmon@ignatius.org
Principal:	William Watts, Ph.D.	Admissions:	Ms. Claire Larmon
# in School:	1,300	# Freshmen:	350
Class Size:	25	Student/Faculty Ratio:	25:1
Tuition:	$7,820/$8,200	Other Expenditures:	

Books: $300
Parent Pledge: contribution to help cover deficit ($25–$10,000)

Profile:
Est. 1870. College prep. Honors and AP courses. Founded originally by members of the Society of Jesus to serve academically talented children of immigrants. Demanding curriculum in the classical Jesuit tradition. Nineteen-acre campus. Known as one of the most prestigious high schools in Chicago.

Public Transportation:
CTA bus: Halsted Street, Roosevelt Road, Blue Island.

Dress Code:
No jeans. Boys: casual slacks, shirt with collar;. Girls: casual slacks or skirt, blouse with sleeves.

Admission Requirements:
Placement exam (taken only at St. Ignatius); transcripts; Catholic heritage and family's history with school taken into consideration.

Scholarships:
N/A

Notes:

Catholic High Schools • Boys

St. Patrick High School
5900 West Belmont Avenue • Chicago, IL 60634
(773) 282-8844 • Fax: (773) 282-3538

Website:	www.stpatrick.org	Email:	jardito@stpatrick.org
Principal:	Mr. Joseph Schmidt	Admissions:	Mr. Jeffrey Ardito
# in School:	980	# Freshmen:	270
Class Size:	28	Student/Faculty Ratio:	20:1
Tuition:	$5,600/$5,900	Other Expenditures:	
			Books: $300

Profile:
Est. 1861. College prep. On existing site since 1953. Chicago's oldest and largest Catholic boys' high school. Founded by the Christian Brothers. Above average student-to-computer ratio. Major million-dollar renovation in 2001.

Public Transportation:
CTA bus:#77 Belmont. St. Patrick bus available at extra cost.

Dress Code:
Dress slacks, collar shirt, no sneakers.

Admission Requirements:
Placement exam.

Scholarships:
Based on placement exam.

Notes:

Catholic High Schools • Boys

St. Rita of Cascia High School
7740 South Western Avenue • Chicago, IL 60620
(773) 925-6600 • Fax: (773) 925-2451

Website:	www.stritahs.com	Email:	mmurtagh@stritahs.com
Principal:	Mr. Joseph F. Bamberger	Admissions:	Mr. Mike Murtagh
# in School:	820	# Freshmen:	200
Class Size:	20	Student/Faculty Ratio:	18:1
Tuition:	$4,850/$5,250	Other Expenditures:	Books: $200

Profile:
Est. 1907. College prep. Augustinian tradition of truth, unity, and charity. Thirty-seven-acre campus. Recognized as a Blue Ribbon School. Listed in *U.S. News and World Report's* "96 Oustanding American High Schools," January, 1999. Recognized as an exemplary school by the U.S. Department of Education.

Public Transportation:
CTA bus: Western Avenue, 79th Street.

Dress Code:
Dress slacks, polo shirt.

Admission Requirements:
Placement exam.

Scholarships:
Based on placement exam: 95 percentile and above = $4,000–$10,000.

Notes:

The Report Card

Catholic High Schools • Girls

St. Scholastica Academy
7416 North Ridge Boulevard • Chicago, IL 60645
(773) 764-5715 • Fax: (773) 764-0304

Website:	www.scholastica.chicago.il.us	**Email:**	hollytobin@yahoo.com
Principal:	Sr. Judith Zonsius, OSB	**Admissions:**	Ms. Holly Tobin
# in School:	325	**# Freshmen:**	75–100
Class Size:	10	**Student/Faculty Ratio:**	12:1
Tuition:	$5,970/$6,170	**Other Expenditures:**	Books: $300

Profile:
Est. 1902. College prep. IB Program (third school in Illinois to be approved). In the tradition of Benedictine values (excellence in a supporting, respectful, caring environment). Fourteen acre campus.

Public Transportation:
CTA el: Red Line to Howard, then bus:#203 Ridge or #97 Skokie.

Dress Code:
Khaki slacks or plaid skirt, polo shirt, sweater.

Admission Requirements:
Placement exam.

Scholarships:
Based on placement exam: 50 percent tuition, $2,000.

Notes:

Catholic High Schools • Girls

Trinity High School
7574 West Division Street • River Forest, IL 60305
(708) 771-8383 • Fax: (708) 488-2014

Website:	www.trinityhs.org	**Email:**	cmulcrone@trinityhs.org
Principal:	Ms. Michele Whitehead	**Admissions:**	Ms. Colleen Mulcrone
# in School:	500	**# Freshmen:**	120
Class Size:	20	**Student/Faculty Ratio:**	13:1
Tuition:	$6,300/$6,750	**Other Expenditures:**	
			Books: $400
			Uniforms: $150

Profile:
Est. 1918. College prep. IB Program. In the Dominican tradition. First Catholic school in Illinois to adopt block scheduling (extended class periods).

Public Transportation:
CTA el: Red and Blue Lines, then Pace bus. Trinity bus available at extra cost.

Dress Code:
Sophomore class votes on uniform; freshmen wear second choice.

Admission Requirements:
Placement exam, transcripts, registration form.

Scholarships:
Based on placement exam: up to $1,500.

Notes:

Catholic High Schools • Girls

Woodlands Academy of the Sacred Heart
760 East Westleigh Road • Lake Forest, IL 60045
(847) 234-4300 • Fax: (847) 234-4348

Website:	www.woodlands.lfc.edu	Email:	kcreed@woodlands.lfc.edu
Principal:	Ms. Madonna Edmunds	Admissions:	Ms. Katie Creed
# in School:	200	# Freshmen:	45–65
Class Size:	15	Student/Faculty Ratio:	9:1
Tuition:	$11,550/$12,765	Other Expenditures:	

General fee: $500
Board 5 days $24,765
Board 7 days $28,030
Learning program: $6,000
English as foreign language: $3,500
Boarder's activity fee: $460–$600
If not available to volunteer: $1,500

Profile:
Est. 1858. College prep. Day and boarding school (1/3 of student population board). Wooded campus in upscale neighborhood next to Barat College. Part of worldwide network of Sacred Heart Schools; also affiliated with National Association of Independent Schools.

Public Transportation:
Within walking distance of the Lake Forest Metra train station.

Dress Code:
Uniform: slacks, skirt, shorts, sweater.

Admission Requirements:
Placement exam, transcripts, essay, interview.

Scholarships:
Based on placement exam: $1,000.

Notes:

The Report Card

INDEPENDENT HIGH SCHOOLS

COED

Chicago Academy for the Arts 34
Chicago Waldorf School 35
Lake Forest Academy 36
Latin School of Chicago 37
Luther High School South..38
Morgan Park Academy...39
North Shore Country Day School 40
Francis W. Parker School 41
Roycemore School 42
The University of Chicago Laboratory Schools 43

Independent High Schools • Coed

Chicago Academy for the Arts
1010 West Chicago Avenue • Chicago, IL 60622
(312) 421-0202 • Fax: (312) 421-3816

Website: chigagoacademyforthearts.org
Principal: Ms. Pamela Johnson
in School: 150
Class Size: 10–20
Tuition: $10,700/$11,325

Email: admissions@chicagoacademyforthearts.org
Admissions: Mr. Mark Taylor
Freshmen: 45
Student/Faculty Ratio: 10:1
Other Expenditures:
New student fee: $150
Activity fee: $275

Profile:
Est. 1980. One of five private high schools for the arts in the country. Non-traditional setting for the talented student. Morning: fully accredited, college prep classes. Afternoon: focus on art form, including history, theory, and technique. Creative facilities include art, dance, and music studios; art gallery; theater.

Public Transportation:
Bus service provided between Northwestern, Union, and LaSalle train stations.

Dress Code:
Appropriate casual, jeans acceptable.

Admission Requirements:
Scholastic ability (test, transcripts); artistic evaluation (audition or portfolio review); personal interview.

Scholarships:
Merit Scholarship based on recommendations, transcripts, and written essay.

Notes:

Independent High Schools • Coed

Chicago Waldorf School
1300 West Loyola Avenue • Chicago, IL 60626
(773) 465-2662 • Fax: (773) 465-6648

Website:	www.chigagowaldorf.org	Email:	info@chicagowaldorf.org
Principal:	Ms. Colleen Everhart (Administrator)	Admissions:	Ms. Marita McLaughlin
# in School:	350	# Freshmen:	15
Class Size:	15	Student/Faculty Ratio:	N/A
Tuition:	$9,900/$10,400	Other Expenditures:	
			Supplies: $995
			Service Learning: $900
			Donation to Waldorf School Assoc.: $60

Profile:
Est. 1974. Pre-school through high school (high school est. 1994). Largest, non-denominational educational movement in the world: 800 schools in 35 countries. Based on a multi-sensory approach to learning that stresses imagination. No formal textbooks are used. Focus is not on computer use or testing.

Public Transportation:
CTA el: Red Line.

Dress Code:
Appropriate casual, jeans acceptable.

Admission Requirements:
Application ($50 fee), transcripts, parent/student interview, math and reading assessment.

Scholarships:
N/A

Notes:

Independent High Schools • Coed

Lake Forest Academy
1500 West Kennedy Road • Lake Forest, IL 60045
(847) 615-3267 • Fax: (847) 615-3202

Website:	www.lfa.lfc.edu	Email:	info@lfa.lfc.edu
Principal:	Dr. John Strudwick	Admissions:	Mr. Christopher Wheeler
# in School:	300	# Freshmen:	80
Class Size:	13	Student/Faculty Ratio:	7:1
Tuition:	$16,000/$17,800	Other Expenditures:	
			Books: $400–$600
			Board: $23,850/$25,500

Profile:
Est. 1857. College prep. AP courses. Performing and fine arts programs. Traditional. Rigorous academic program. Small class size. Fifty percent of students (from 13 countries, 16 states) board at school. Set on 160 acres (former estate of Ogden Armour) with ponds, woods, and open space in the affluent Lake Forest.

Public Transportation:
School bus pick-up from train stations.

Dress Code:
No denim or sneakers. Boys: dress slacks, button-down dress shirt, tie; girls: dress, skirt, slacks, blouse.

Admission Requirements:
Placement exam, application, transcripts.

Scholarships:
Merit grants based on exam and transcripts: $4,000 ($6,000 to board). transcripts.

Notes:

Independent High Schools • Coed

Latin School of Chicago
59 West North Avenue • Chicago, IL 60610
(312) 573-4600 • Fax: (312) 573-0328

Website:	www.latinschool.org	**Email:**	jbail@latinschool.org
Principal:	Mr. Frank Hogan	**Admissions:**	Ms. Janice G. Bail
# in School:	1,080	**# Freshmen:**	100
Class Size:	15	**Student/Faculty Ratio:**	8:1
Tuition:	$16,300/$17,400	**Other Expenditures:**	

Books: $400–$600
Annual Fund: $1,000;
$500 additional child
Capital Improvement Assessment Donation

Profile:
Est. 1888. Junior kindergarten through high school. College prep. Prestigious and traditional. Rigorous academic program. AP courses. Member of School Year Abroad Consortium. Independent Study Program. Separate building for middle and high school.

Public Transportation:
CTA el: Red and Brown Lines; bus: Clark Street #22, Broadway #36, Lincoln Avenue #11, North Avenue #72.

Dress Code:
Appropriate casual, jeans acceptable.

Admission Requirements:
Application ($40 fee); recommendation from principal and English and math teachers; transcripts; ISEE exam. Preference to siblings and children of alumni.

Scholarships:
N/A

Notes:

Independent High Schools • Coed

Luther High School South
3130 West 87 Street • Chicago, IL 60652
(773) 737-1416 • Fax: (773) 737-2882

Website:	www.luthersouth.com	Email:	see website
Principal:	Mr. Paul Enderie	Admissions:	Ms. Tiffany Shanks
# in School:	240	# Freshmen:	75–90
Class Size:	15–25	Student/Faculty Ratio:	14:1
Tuition:	$5,145/$5,345	Other Expenditures:	
			Books: $200

Profile:
College prep. AP courses. Established in the Lutheran tradition (ethical, moral values).

Public Transportation:
CTA bus: Kedzie Avenue/87th Street.

Dress Code:
Appropriate casual, jeans acceptable.

Admission Requirements:
Placement exam, transcripts.

Scholarships:
Based on entrance exam.

Notes:

Independent High Schools • Coed

Morgan Park Academy
2153 West 111th Street • Chicago, IL 60643
(773) 881-6700 • Fax: (773) 881-8409

Website: www.morganparkacademy.org	Email:sgrassi@morganparkacedemy.org
Principal: Mr. David Hibbs	Admissions: Ms. Sara Grassi
# in School: 545	# Freshmen: 50
Class Size: 5–18	Student/Faculty Ratio: 10:1
Tuition: $11,600/$12,300	Other Expenditures:
	Books: $350–$500

Profile:
Est. 1873. Pre-school through high school. College prep. Multi-cultural and socio-economic student mix. Hands-on approach, with emphasis on the individual. Twenty-acre Ivy League campus located in the Beverly/Morgan Park area.

Public Transportation:
Metra Train: 111th Street/Western Avenue. School bus service available.

Dress Code:
Appropriate casual, jeans acceptable.

Admission Requirements:
Placement exam, transcripts.

Scholarships:
Honors scholarship based on portfolio and entrance exam: up to 50 percent off all four years.

Notes:

Independent High Schools • Coed

North Shore Country Day School
310 Green Bay Road • Winnetka, IL 60093
(847) 446-0674 • Fax: (847) 446-0675

Website:	www.nscds.org	Email:	dwentz@nsscds.org
Principal:	Mr. Tom Doar	Admissions:	Mr. Dale Wentz
# in School:	450	# Freshmen:	40
Class Size:	13	Student/Faculty Ratio:	7:1
Tuition:	$15,074/$15,100		Other Expenditures:
10th, 11th, 12th grades: $16,100			Books: $250–$300
			Annual Giving Fund Donation

Profile:
Est. 1919. Kindergarten through high school. College prep. AP courses. Independent study courses. Rigorous academic program. Located on sixteen acres in affluent Winnetka. Appointed to the Independent School Consortium on Innovation.

Public Transportation:
Within walking distance of Metra Train station.

Dress Code:
Appropriate casual, jeans acceptable.

Admission Requirements:
ISEE exam, transcripts.

Scholarships:
Scholarship for Excellence exam results, interviews, teacher recommendations, transcripts. One merit-based scholarship awarded and renewed on annual basis after academic review.

Notes:

Independent High Schools • Coed

Francis W. Parker School
330 West Webster Avenue • Chicago, IL 60614
(773) 353-3000 • Fax: (773) 549-0587

Website:	www.fwparker.org	Email:	admissions@fwparker.org
Principal:	Mr. Donald S. Monroe	Admissions:	Ms. Elizabeth Cicchelli
# in School:	875	# Freshmen:	80
Class Size:	15	Student/Faculty Ratio:	18:1
Tuition:	$15,030/$15,857	Other Expenditures:	
		Fair Share Fund: $1,350 per year	

Profile:
Est. 1907 by Colonel Francis Parker and based upon John Dewey's educational theory of complete mental, physical, and moral development of the individual. Junior kindergarten through high school. College prep. AP courses. Prestigious. Located on Chicago's north side, in Lincoln Park.

Public Transportation:
CTA bus: #22 Clark Street, #36 Broadway, #151 Sheridan Road, #156 LaSalle Street.

Dress Code:
Appropriate casual, jeans acceptable.

Admission Requirements:
Application ($50 fee); ISEE exam; parent interview; recommendations from principal and English and math teachers; transcripts.

Scholarships:
N/A

Notes:

Independent High Schools • Coed

Roycemore School
640 Lincoln Street • Evanston, IL 60201
(847) 866-6055 • (847) 866-6545

Website:	www.roycemoreschool.org	Email:	bturnbull@roycemoreschool.org
Principal:	Mr. Frank Spica	Admissions:	Ms. Barbara Turnbull
# in School:	250	# Freshmen:	25
Class Size:	10	Student/Faculty Ratio:	10:1
Tuition:	$14,750/$15,340	Other Expenditures:	
		Books, field trips, lunches: $1,690	

Profile:
Est. 1915. Junior kindergarten through high school. College prep. AP courses. Course affiliation with Northwestern University. January term is shortened so students may carry out independent projects at school, in the area, or the world. National Historic Register building.

Public Transportation:
CTA el: Purple Line/Noyes.

Dress Code:
Appropriate casual, jeans acceptable.

Admission Requirements:
No placement exam, transcripts, recommendations, writing sample.

Scholarships:
Full tuition merit scholarships based on recommendations, transcripts, 95th percentile rank.

Notes:

Independent High Schools • Coed

The University of Chicago Laboratory Schools
1362 East 59th Street • Chicago, IL 60637
(773) 702-9450 • (773) 702-7455

Website:	www.ucls.uchicago.edu	Email:	admissions@ucls.uchicago.edu
Principal:	Mr. Jack Knapp	Admissions:	Ms. Alice Haskell
# in School:	1,675	# Freshmen:	120
Class Size:	17	Student/Faculty Ratio:	N/A
Tuition:	$14,328/$15,201	Other Expenditures:	Books: $400

Profile:
Est. 1896. Pre-school through high school. Founded by education philosopher John Dewey and based upon his educational theory of complete mental, physical, and moral development of the individual. College prep. Thirty to 35 percent of each year's graduating class are National Merit Scholarship semi-finalists. Hyde Park neighborhood.

Public Transportation:
CTA bus: #6 Jeffrey Express/Hyde Park; IC Train/59th Street.

Dress Code:
Appropriate casual, jeans acceptable.

Admission Requirements:
Application ($75 fee); ISEE exam; school recommendations; parent interview.

Scholarships:
N/A

Notes:

The Report Card

PUBLIC HIGH SCHOOLS

COED

Amundsen High School 48
Austin Community Academy 49
Best Practice High School 50
Bogan Technical High School 51
James H. Bowen High School 52
Gwendolyn Brooks College Preparatory Academy 53
Calumet Career Preparatory Academy 54
Carver Military Academy 55
Chicago High School for Agricultural Sciences 56
Chicago International Charter High School 57
Chicago Military Academy – Bronzeville 58
Chicago Vocational Career Academy 59
Clemente Community Academy 60
George Washington Collins High School 61
George Henry Corliss High School 62
Crane Technical Preparatory Common School 63
Maria Sklodowska Curie Metropolitan High School 64
Dunbar Vocational Career Academy 65
DuSable High School 66
Englewood Technical High School 67
Farragut Career Academy 68
Fenger Academy High School 69
Flower Career Academy 70
Foreman High School 71
Gage Park High School 72
Hancock High School 73
Harlan Community Academy 74
Harper High School 75
Hirsch Metropolitan High School 76
John Hope College Preparatory High School 77

Hubbard High School	78
Hyde Park Academy High School	79
Jones Academic Magnet College Preparatory High School	80
Benito Juarez Community Academy	81
Percy L. Julian High School	82
Thomas Kelly High School	83
Kelvyn Park High School	84
Kennedy High School	85
Kenwood Academy High School	86
Dr. Martin Luther King High School	87
Lake View High School	88
Lane Technical College Preparatory High School	89
Lincoln Park High School	90
Lindblom College Preparatory High School	91
Manley Career Academy	92
Marshall Metropolitan High School	93
Mather High School	94
Morgan Park High School	95
Noble Street Charter High School	96
North Lawndale College Preparatory Charter High School	97
Northside College Preparatory High School	98
Rezin Orr Community Academy High School	99
Walter Payton College Preparatory High School	100
Perspectives Charter High School	101
Phillips Academy	102
Prosser Career Academy High School	103
Richards Career Academy	104
Paul Robeson High School	105
Roosevelt High School	106
Schurz High School	107
Senn Metropolitan High School	108
Simeon Vocational Career Academy	109
South Shore Community Academy	110
Jesse Spaulding High School	111
Steinmetz Academic Centre	112
Sullivan High School	113

William Howard Taft High School 114
Tilden Community Career Academy 115
Von Steuben Metropolitan Science Center 116
Washington High School 117
Wells Community Academy High School 118
Westinghouse Career Academy 119
Whitney M. Young Magnet High School 121
Youth Connection Charter High School (Headquarters) 122

GIRLS

Young Women's Leadership Charter School 120

Public High Schools • Coed

Amundsen High School
5110 North Damen Avenue • Chicago, IL 60625
(773) 534-2320 • Fax: (773) 534-2428

Website:	www.amundsen.edu	Email:	See website
Principal:	Dr. Pauline A. Tarvardian	Admissions:	Ms. Jessica Azcoitia
# in School:	1,600	# Freshmen:	475
Class Size:	25–28	Student/Faculty Ratio:	18:1
Tuition:	N/A	Other Expenditures:	N/A

Profile:
Region 1. Magnet school. College prep. IB program.* Honors and AP courses. School within a school. Ethnically diverse (English is not the first language for 70 percent of the student body). Award-winning landscape cultivated by student body.

Public Transportation:
CTA bus: Damen/Foster Avenues.

Dress Code:
Appropriate casual, jeans acceptable.

Admission Requirements:
Students must reside in Region 1.* Students living outside of Region 1 may apply (separate application required).

Scholarships:
N/A

Notes:

Austin Community Academy
231 North Pine Avenue • Chicago, IL 60644
(773) 534-6300 • Fax: (773) 534-6046

Website:	www.cps.k12.il.us	Email:	See website
Principal:	Ms. Learna Brewer-Baker	Admissions:	Ms. Jane Weiss
# in School:	1,160	# Freshmen:	500
Class Size:	27	Student/Faculty Ratio:	16:1
Tuition:	N/A	Other Expenditures:	N/A

Profile:
Region 3. Magnet school. Prospective IB program.* Honors and AP courses. ETC Program: performing arts, culinary arts, hotel management, automotive technology, computer network design, Sheriff Academy, Business Academy, JROTC.

Public Transportation:
CTA el: Lake Street; bus: Central, Madison.

Dress Code:
Solid black slacks or skirt, solid white top.

Admission Requirements:
Students must reside in Region 3. *IB = minimum stanine of six, parent-student interview, writing sample, solid academic performance.

Scholarships:
N/A

Notes:

Public High Schools • Coed

Best Practice High School
2040 West Adams Street • Chicago, IL 60612
(773) 534-7610 • Fax: (773) 534-7601

Website:	www.cps.k12.il.us	Email:	See website
Principal:	Mr. Richard Gray	Admissions:	Ms. Aiko Boyce
# in School:	400	# Freshmen:	100
Class Size:	28	Student/Faculty Ratio:	20:1
Tuition:	N/A	Other Expenditures:	N/A

Profile:
Region 3. College prep. AP courses. Small-school concept. Mostly African-American and Latin student population. Bilingual staff: Spanish. Students assist in planning curriculum.

Public Transportation:
CTA el: Red and Blue Lines. (near United Center).

Dress Code:
Appropriate casual, jeans acceptable.

Admission Requirements:
Accepts students citywide: application, placement exam.

Scholarships:
N/A

Notes:

Bogan Technical High School

3939 West 79th Street • Chicago, IL 60652
(773) 535-2180 • Fax: (773) 535-2165

Website:	www.cps.k12.il.us	Email:	See website
Principal:	Mr. Robert Miller	Admissions:	Mr. Ed Kilcoyne
# in School:	2,000	# Freshmen:	500
Class Size:	28	Student/Faculty Ratio:	21:1
Tuition:	N/A	Other Expenditures:	N/A

Profile:
Region 5. Magnet school. Prospective IB program.* Technology Academy. Options for Knowledge school (computers). International Language Academy: Spanish. Career Academy: international business. ETC Program: CISCO, finance/accounting, Chicago police and firefighting training, nursing. Featured as one of the Top Wired Schools in *Family PC Magazine*.

Public Transportation:
CTA el: Orange Line, near Pulaski.

Dress Code:
Solid black slacks or skirt, solid white top, solid black shoes.

Admission Requirements:
Accepts students citywide: application; lottery selection. *IB = minimum stanine of six, parent-student interview, writing sample, solid academic performance.

Scholarships:
N/A

Notes:

Public High Schools • Coed

James H. Bowen High School
2710 East 89th Street • Chicago, IL 60617
(773) 535-6000 • Fax: (773) 535-6034

Website:	www.cps.k12.il.us	Email:	See website
Principal:	Mr. Fausto Lopez	Admissions:	Mr. Michael Kenney
# in School:	950	# Freshmen:	300
Class Size:	28	Student/Faculty Ratio:	11:1
Tuition:	N/A	Other Expenditures:	N/A

Profile:
Region 6. College prep. AP courses. School within a school. School to Work Program. Information Technology Program.

Public Transportation:
CTA bus: 87th Street/South Chicago Avenue.

Dress Code:
Blue or black slacks or skirt, white top.

Admission Requirements:
Students must reside in Region 6.

Scholarships:
N/A

Notes:

Public High Schools • Coed

Gwendolyn Brooks College Preparatory Academy
(Formerly Southside College Preparatory Academy)
250 East 111th Street • Chicago, IL 60628
(773) 535-9930 • Fax: (773) 535-9939

Website:	www.cps.k12.il.us	Email:	See website
Principal:	Ms. Linda C. Layne	Admissions:	Ms. Siobhan M. Cafferty
# in School:	500	# Freshmen:	150 - 175
Class Size:	28	Student/Faculty Ratio:	15:1
Tuition:	N/A	Other Expenditures:	N/A

Profile:
Region 6. Magnet school. College prep. Serving Chicago's south side. Selective Enrollment School. Rigorous academic program.

Public Transportation:
CTA bus: King Drive.

Dress Code:
Blue slacks or skirt, white collar top.

Admission Requirements:
Selective Enrollment Application. Minimum stanine of five in reading and math on 7th grade standardized tests.

Scholarships:
N/A

Notes:

The Report Card

Public High Schools • Coed

Calumet Career Preparatory Academy
8131 South May Street • Chicago, IL 60620
(773) 535-3500 • Fax: (773) 535-3513

Website:	www.cps.k12.il.us	Email:	See website
Principal:	Ms. Daya Locke	Admissions:	Mr. John Wheatley
# in School:	950	# Freshmen:	500
Class Size:	28	Student/Faculty Ratio:	N/A
Tuition:	N/A	Other Expenditures:	N/A

Profile:
Region 5. Magnet school. School within a school. JROTC Academy (Army). Law and Public Safety Academy. Career Academy: communications, construction, health, hospitality, performing arts.

Public Transportation:
CTA bus: Racine.

Dress Code:
JROTC: blue and white uniform, dress uniform—weekly inspections, special ceremonies.
Non-JROTC: blue slacks or skirt, white top.

Admission Requirements:
Students must reside in Region 5. Separate application, transcripts.

Scholarships:
N/A

Notes:

Public High Schools • Coed

Carver Military Academy
13100 South Doty Road • Chicago, IL 60827
(773) 535-5250 • Fax: (773) 535-5037

Website:	www.cps.k12.il.us	Email:	See website
Principal:	Dr. William Johnson	Admissions:	Ms. Kathryn Alderson
# in School:	725	# Freshmen:	250
Class Size:	28	Student/Faculty Ratio:	14:1
Tuition:	N/A	Other Expenditures:	N/A

Profile:
Region 6. Magnet school. AP courses. Scholars program. Full site JROTC Academy (Army). One of the first public schools in the nation to convert to a military academy. ETC Program: performing arts/theater, nursing, Chicago police and firefighter training.

Public Transportation:
CTA bus: 130th Street.

Dress Code:
Government standard military uniform.

Admission Requirements:
Accepts students citywide. Separate application required: interview, transcripts, letter of recommendation and signed ROTC contract.

Scholarships:
N/A

Notes:

Public High Schools • Coed

Chicago High School for Agricultural Sciences
3857 West 111th Street • Chicago, IL 60655
(773) 535-2500 • Fax: (773) 535-2507

Website:	www.cps.k12.il.us	Email:	See website
Principal:	Mr. David Gilligan	Admissions:	Mr. Luis Maturana
# in School:	600	# Freshmen:	150
Class Size:	25	Student/Faculty Ratio:	24:1
Tuition:	N/A	Other Expenditures:	N/A

Profile:
Region 6. Magnet school. AP courses. Agricultural science and business. Seventy-two-acre land lab located on the last existing farm in Chicago. Innovative, hands-on curriculum for talented science and math students. Only school of its kind in the Midwest. Named a "New American High School" by the U.S. Department of Education. Serves as a model for other like schools across the U.S. Summer employment and internship programs at the University of Illinois and Michigan State.

Public Transportation:
CTA bus: Pulaski Road/111th Street.

Dress Code:
Appropriate casual, jeans acceptable.

Admission Requirements:
Accepts students citywide: minimum stanine of five in reading and math on most recent standardized test, interview; lottery selection.

Scholarships:
N/A

Notes:

Chicago International Charter High School

1309 West 95th Street • Chicago, IL 60643
(773) 238-5330 • Fax: (773) 238-5350

Website:	www.cps.k12.il.us	Email:	See website
Principal:	Mr. Robert Lang	Admissions:	Ms. Tinille Jackson
# in School:	1,250	# Freshmen:	70
Class Size:	25–30	Student/Faculty Ratio:	N/A
Tuition:	N/A	Other Expenditures:	N/A

Profile:
Region 6. College prep. Multi-campus charter school run by the Chicago Charter School Foundation. Rigorous academic program. Nationally recognized educational program.

Public Transportation:
CTA bus: Dan Ryan Station, 95th Street, State Street; Metra Train: Vincennes Avenue.

Dress Code:
Gray slacks, white shirt, burgundy sweater.

Admission Requirements:
Accepts students citywide.

Scholarships:
N/A

Notes:

Public High Schools • Coed

Chicago Military Academy–Bronzeville
3519 South Giles Street • Chicago, IL 60653
(773) 534-9750 • Fax: (773) 534-9768

Website:	www.cps.k12.il.us	Email:	See website
Principal:	Ms. Phyllis Goodson	Admissions:	Ms. Cheryl Phillips
# in School:	300	# Freshmen:	170
Class Size:	24	Student/Faculty Ratio:	24:1
Tuition:	N/A	Other Expenditures:	N/A

Profile:
Region 4. Magnet school. College prep. Full site JROTC Academy (Army).

Public Transportation:
CTA bus: King Drive.

Dress Code:
Government standard military uniform.

Admission Requirements:
Students must reside in Region 4. Separate application required: interview, transcripts, letter of recommendation and signed ROTC contract.

Scholarships:
N/A

Notes:

Chicago Vocational Career Academy

2100 East 87th Street • Chicago, IL 60617
(773) 535-6100 • Fax: (773) 535-6633

Website:	www.cps.k12.il.us	Email:	See website
Principal:	Mr. Ronald Beavers	Admissions:	Ms. Michelle Roedel
# in School:	2,400	# Freshmen:	600–800
Class Size:	25	Student/Faculty Ratio:	20:1
Tuition:	N/A	Other Expenditures:	N/A

Profile:
Region 6. Magnet school. College and career prep. AP courses. School within a school: JROTC Academy (Army). Career Academy: business/finance, communications, construction, cosmetology, health, hospitality, manufacturing, performing arts, transportation. Named one of five New Urban High Schools (for cutting edge programs) and one of twelve Entrepreneurial Schools in the nation by the U.S. Department of Education.

Public Transportation:
CTA bus: 87th/Jeffrey Streets.

Dress Code:
Blue slacks, skirt, or shorts; white, navy, or gold polo shirt; no jeans.

Admission Requirements:
Accepts students citywide: separate application required, minimum stanine of five in reading and math required on most recent standardized test.

Scholarships:
N/A

Notes:

Public High Schools • Coed

Clemente Community Academy
1147 North Western Avenue • Chicago, IL 60622
(773) 534-4000 • Fax: (773) 534-4012

Website:	www.cps.k12.il.us	Email:	See website
Principal:	Ms. Irene DeMota	Admissions:	Ms. Martha Trueheart
# in School:	1,800	# Freshmen:	650
Class Size:	28	Student/Faculty Ratio:	17:1
Tuition:	N/A	Other Expenditures:	N/A

Profile:
Region 2. Magnet school. College and career prep. Honors and AP courses. Math, Science, and Technology Academy.* International Language Academy: Spanish, French. Career Academy: culinary arts. ETC Program: CISCO, culinary arts, fashion design, architectural drafting, earth and spatial technology, JROTC, business.

Public Transportation:
CTA bus: Division, Western Avenues.

Dress Code:
Blue or black slacks, white shirt.

Admission Requirements:
Accepts students citywide (priority given to students who reside in Region 2). *Separate application required.

Scholarships:
N/A

Notes:

Public High Schools • Coed

George Washington Collins High School
1313 South Sacramento Boulevard • Chicago, IL 60623
(773) 534-1500 • Fax: (773) 534-1399

Website:	www.cps.k12.il.us	Email:	See website
Principal:	Dr. Diane Dyer-Dawson	Admissions:	Mr. Michael Clark
# in School:	800	# Freshmen:	225
Class Size:	22	Student/Faculty Ratio:	17:1
Tuition:	N/A	Other Expenditures:	N/A

Profile:
Region 3. Magnet school. College and career prep. Serving the Lawndale community. AP courses. Prospective IB program.* ETC Program: automotive technology, culinary arts, information processing, JROTC.

Public Transportation:
CTA bus: Roosevelt Road.

Dress Code:
Appropriate casual, no jeans.

Admission Requirements:
Students must reside in Region 3. * Separate application required.

Scholarships:
N/A

Notes:

The Report Card

Public High Schools • Coed

George Henry Corliss High School
821 East 103rd Street • Chicago, IL 60668
(773) 535-5115 • Fax: (773) 535-5511

Website:	www.cps.k12.il.us	Email:	See website
Principal:	Mr. Anthony Spivey	Admissions:	Ms. Shari Stennis
# in School:	1,000	# Freshmen:	325
Class Size:	28	Student/Faculty Ratio:	17:1
Tuition:	N/A	Other Expenditures:	N/A

Profile:
Region 6. Magnet school: fine and performing arts program (band). College and career prep. AP courses. Options for Knowledge School (fine arts, humanities). Academy of Finance. ETC Program: accounting, business, carpentry, computer, commercial art, culinary arts, graphic design, information processing.

Public Transportation:
CTA bus: 106th, 108th Streets.

Dress Code:
Black slacks or skirt, white collar shirt.

Admission Requirements:
Students must reside in Region 6.

Scholarships:
N/A

Notes:

Crane Technical Preparatory Common School

2245 West Jackson Boulevard • Chicago, IL 60612
(773) 534-7550 • Fax: (773) 534-7557

Website:	www.cps.k12.il.us	Email:	See website
Principal:	Mr. Melver L. Scott	Admissions:	Ms. Betty Fuller
# in School:	1,110	# Freshmen:	400
Class Size:	28	Student/Faculty Ratio:	16:1
Tuition:	N/A	Other Expenditures:	N/A

Profile:
Region 3. Magnet school. College and career prep. AP courses. Math, Science, and Technology Academy.* Technology Academy. ETC Program: travel and tourism, automotive technology, business/finance, health and nursing, performing arts, culinary arts.

Public Transportation:
CTA el: Western Avenue; bus: Jackson Boulevard.

Dress Code:
Appropriate casual, jeans acceptable.

Admission Requirements:
Accepts students citywide; priority given to those students who reside in Region 3. *Separate application required.

Scholarships:
N/A

Notes:

Public High Schools • Coed

Marie Sklodowska Curie Metropolitan High School
4959 South Archer Avenue • Chicago, IL 60632
(773) 535-2100 • Fax: (773) 535-2049

Website:	www.cps.k12.il.us	Email:	See website
Principal:	Ms. Jerrlyn Jones	Admissions:	Ms. Anna Espinosa
# in School:	3,000	# Freshmen:	700–950
Class Size:	30	Student/Faculty Ratio:	25:1
Tuition:	N/A	Other Expenditures:	N/A

Profile:
Region 4. Magnet school: fine and performing arts program.* AP courses. Participating IB program.** Career Academy: communications, construction, health, hospitality, performing arts.**

Public Transportation:
CTA el: Orange Line.

Dress Code:
Appropriate casual, jeans acceptable.

Admission Requirements:
Students must reside in mandatory area within Region 4. Separate application required. *Final selection based on lottery. **Interview and minimum stanine of seven on most recent standardized tests in area of career interest.

Scholarships:
N/A

Notes:

Public High Schools • Coed

Dunbar Vocational Career Academy
3000 South King Drive • Chicago, IL 60616
(773) 534-9000 • Fax: (773) 534-9250

Website:	www.cps.k12.il.us	Email:	See website
Principal:	Dr. Barbara Hall	Admissions:	Mr. Reginald Gayles
# in School:	1,800	# Freshmen:	500
Class Size:	30	Student/Faculty Ratio:	23:1
Tuition:	N/A	Other Expenditures:	N/A

Profile:
Region 4. Est. 2001. Magnet school. College and career prep. School within a school. Mostly African-American student body. Career Academy:* business/finance, communications, construction, cosmetology, health, hospitality, manufacturing, and transportation.

Public Transportation:
CTA el: State Street/King Drive; bus: 29th/State Street.

Dress Code:
Appropriate casual, no jeans.

Admission Requirements:
Accepts students citywide. *Separate application required.

Scholarships:
N/A

Notes:

Public High Schools • Coed

DuSable High School
4934 South Wabash Avenue • Chicago, IL 60615
(773) 535-1100 • Fax: (773) 535-1004

Website:	www.cps.k12.il.us	Email:	See website
Principal:	Dr. Gloria Archbold	Admissions:	Ms. Delores Beasley
# in School:	625	# Freshmen:	225
Class Size:	28	Student/Faculty Ratio:	14:1
Tuition:	N/A	Other Expenditures:	N/A

Profile:
Region 4. Magnet school. College and career prep. Options for Knowledge Program.* ETC Program: JROTC, culinary arts, construction, medical technician, nursing. Mostly African-American student population. Prestigious alumnae include Mayor Harold Washington and Mr. John Johnson, publisher of *Ebony Magazine*.

Public Transportation:
CTA bus: State Street.

Dress Code:
Appropriate casual, no jeans.

Admission Requirements:
Students must reside in Region 4. *Application required; lottery selection.

Scholarships:
N/A

Notes:

Public High Schools • Coed

Englewood Technical High School
6201 South Stewart Avenue • Chicago, IL 60621
(773) 535-3600 • Fax: (773) 535-3586

Website:	www.cps.k12.il.us	Email:	See website
Principal:	Ms. Diane L. Jackson	Admissions:	Mr. Rai Flowers
# in School:	900	# Freshmen:	500
Class Size:	25	Student/Faculty Ratio:	13:1
Tuition:	N/A	Other Expenditures:	N/A

Profile:
Region 5. Technical Preparatory Academy. State-of-the-art science lab. One of the city's few fully air conditioned schools. Named one of the safest schools in Region 5.

Public Transportation:
CTA el: Green line/63rd Street.

Dress Code:
Appropriate casual, no jeans.

Admission Requirements:
Students must reside in Region 5. Transcripts.

Scholarships:
N/A

Notes:

Public High Schools • Coed

Farragut Career Academy
2345 South Christiana Avenue • Chicago, IL 60623
(773) 534-1300 • Fax: (773) 534-1336

Website:	www.cps.k12.il.us	Email:	See website
Principal:	Mr. Edward Guerra	Admissions:	Mr. Daniel Boni
# in School:	2,200	# Freshmen:	500–900
Class Size:	28	Student/Faculty Ratio:	22:1
Tuition:	N/A	Other Expenditures:	N/A

Profile:
Region 4. Magnet school. College and career prep. Serving the Little Village and North Lawndale communities. School within a school. JROTC Program (Army). Technology Academy. Career Academy: construction, health, hospitality, manufacturing, transportation.

Public Transportation:
CTA el: Red line; bus: #60.

Dress Code:
Black slacks or skirt, white top.

Admission Requirements:
Students must reside in Region 4.

Scholarships:
N/A

Notes:

Fenger Academy High School

11220 South Wallace Street • Chicago, IL 60628
(773) 535-5430 • Fax: (773) 535-5444

Website:	www.cps.k12.il.us	Email:	See website
Principal:	Ms. Janet Ollarvia	Admissions:	Ms. Sandra Slone
# in School:	900	# Freshmen:	350
Class Size:	28	Student/Faculty Ratio:	18:1
Tuition:	N/A	Other Expenditures:	N/A

Profile:
Region 6. Magnet school. Math, Science, and Technology Academy.* Technology Academy.

Public Transportation:
CTA bus: Halsted, 111th, 115th Streets.

Dress Code:
Black slacks or skirt, white top.

Admission Requirements:
*Priority given to students who reside in Region 6.

Scholarships:
N/A

Notes:

Public High Schools • Coed

Flower Career Academy
3545 West Fulton Boulevard • Chicago, IL 60624
(773) 534-6755 • Fax: (773) 534-6938

Website:	www.cps.k12.il.us	Email:	See website
Principal:	Ms. Dorothy Williams	Admissions:	Ms. Newsome-Weatherspoon
# in School:	500	# Freshmen:	Accepted in 2003
Class Size:	28	Student/Faculty Ratio:	17:1
Tuition:	N/A	Other Expenditures:	N/A

Profile:
Region 3. Career Academy: business/finance, construction, manufacturing. Reopening planned September 2002; vocational programs to open in stages.

Public Transportation:
CTA el: Green Line/Central Park.

Dress Code:
Appropriate casual, no jeans.

Admission Requirements:
Accepts students citywide. Separate application required.

Scholarships:
N/A

Notes:

Public High Schools • Coed

Foreman High School
3235 North Leclaire Avenue • Chicago, IL 60641
(773) 534-3400 • Fax: (773) 534-3684

Website:	www.cps.k12.il.us	Email:	See website
Principal:	Mr. Frank Candioto	Admissions:	Ms. Nila King
# in School:	1,600	# Freshmen:	500
Class Size:	28	Student/Faculty Ratio:	17:1
Tuition:	N/A	Other Expenditures:	N/A

Profile:
Region 1. Bilingual: Spanish, Polish. AP courses. ETC Program: word processing, electronics, graphic design. CPS Scholars Program.

Public Transportation:
CTA bus: Belmont.

Dress Code:
Black, beige, or blue slacks or skirt; white top.

Admission Requirements:
Students must reside in Region 1.

Scholarships:
N/A

Notes:

Public High Schools • Coed

Gage Park High School
5630 South Rockwell Street • Chicago, IL 60629
(773) 535-9230 • Fax: (773) 535-9411

Website:	www.cps.k12.il.us	Email:	See website
Principal:	Dr. Katherine O. Smith	Admissions:	Ms. Karen January
# in School:	1,500	# Freshmen:	600
Class Size:	28	Student/Faculty Ratio:	22:1
Tuition:	N/A	Other Expenditures:	N/A

Profile:
Region 5. School within a school. PRIDE Program. Mostly Latin-American student population.

Public Transportation:
CTA bus: 55th Street.

Dress Code:
Black slacks or skirt, white top.

Admission Requirements:
Students must reside in Region 5.

Scholarships:
N/A

Notes:

The Report Card

Public High Schools • Coed

Hancock High School
4350 West 79th Street • Chicago, IL 60629
(773) 535-2410 • Fax: (773) 535-2434

Website:	www.cps.k12.il.us	Email:	See website
Principal:	Mr. James Iles	Admissions:	Mr. James Iles
# in School:	400	# Freshmen:	200*
Class Size:	28	Student/Faculty Ratio:	17:1
Tuition:	N/A	Other Expenditures:	N/A

Profile: Region 5. School within a school. Enlarging campus.*

Public Transportation:
CTA bus: 79th Street/Cicero Avenue.

Dress Code:
Appropriate casual, jeans acceptable; white shirt with collar.

Admission Requirements:
Accepts students citywide.

Scholarships:
N/A

Notes:

The Report Card

Public High Schools • Coed

Harlan Community Academy
9625 South Michigan Avenue • Chicago, IL 60628
(773) 535-5400 • Fax: (773) 535-5061

Website:	www.cps.k12.il.us	Email:	See website
Principal:	Ms. Patricia Grissett	Admissions:	Ms. Susan Lawrence
# in School:	700	# Freshmen:	275
Class Size:	28	Student/Faculty Ratio:	12:1
Tuition:	N/A	Other Expenditures:	N/A

Profile:
Region 6. Magnet school. Math, Science, and Technology Academy. Options for Knowledge Program.*

Public Transportation:
CTA bus: Michigan Avenue.

Dress Code:
Appropriate casual, jeans acceptable.

Admission Requirements:
Priority given to students who reside in Region 6. *Application required; lottery selection.

Scholarships:
N/A

Notes:

Public High Schools • Coed

Harper High School
6520 South Wood Street • Chicago, IL 60636
(773) 535-9150 • Fax: (773) 535-9090

Website:	www.cps.k12.il.us	Email:	See website
Principal:	Mr. Kent Nolan	Admissions:	Ms. Romell Walton
# in School:	1,400	# Freshmen:	500
Class Size:	25–30	Student/Faculty Ratio:	15:1
Tuition:	N/A	Other Expenditures:	N/A

Profile:
Region 5. Magnet school. International Language Academy: Spanish, French. Career Academy: travel and tourism. Options for Knowledge Program.*

Public Transportation:
CTA bus: 63rd Street.

Dress Code:
Black slacks or skirt, white top.

Admission Requirements:
Priority given to students who reside in Region 5. *Application required; lottery selection.

Scholarships:
N/A

Notes:

Public High Schools • Coed

Hirsch Metropolitan High School
7740 South Ingleside Avenue • Chicago, IL 60619
(773) 535-3100 • Fax: (773) 535-3240

Website:	www.cps.k12.il.us	Email:	See website
Principal:	Dr. M.D. Parker	Admissions:	Ms. Linda Bailey
# in School:	600	# Freshmen:	150
Class Size:	20 - 24	Student/Faculty Ratio:	16:1
Tuition:	N/A	Other Expenditures:	N/A

Profile:
Region 5. Magnet school. Law and Public Safety Academies.

Public Transportation:
CTA bus: Cottage Grove Boulevard.

Dress Code:
Appropriate casual, no jeans.

Admission Requirements:
Accepts students citywide.

Scholarships:
N/A

Notes:

Public High Schools • Coed

John Hope College Preparatory High School
5515 Lowe Street • Chicago, IL 60621
(773) 535-3160 • Fax: (773) 535-3444

Website:	www.cps.k12.il.us	Email:	See website
Principal:	Dr. Mahalia Hiner	Admissions:	Ms. Shawn Lambkin
# in School:	1,000	# Freshmen:	150
Class Size:	26	Student/Faculty Ratio:	N/A
Tuition:	N/A	Other Expenditures:	N/A

Profile:
Region 5. Magnet school. College prep.

Public Transportation:
CTA bus: Garfield.

Dress Code:
Khaki slacks, white or blue shirt.

Admission Requirements:
Accepts students citywide. Separate application required.

Scholarships:
N/A

Notes:

Public High Schools • Coed

Hubbard High School

6200 South Hamlin Avenue • Chicago, IL 60629
(773) 535-2200 • Fax: (773) 535-2218

Website:	www.cps.k12.il.us	**Email:**	See website
Principal:	Ms. Valerie Doubrawa	**Admissions:**	Ms. Christine Alexander
# in School:	1,700	**# Freshmen:**	400
Class Size:	25	**Student/Faculty Ratio:**	21:1
Tuition:	N/A	**Other Expenditures:**	N/A

Profile:
Region 5. Magnet school. College prep. AP courses. IB program.*

Public Transportation:
CTA el: Orange Line; bus: Pulaski, 63rd Streets.

Dress Code:
Black slacks or skirt, white shirt.

Admission Requirements:
Priority given to students who reside in Region 5. *Separate application required.

Scholarships:
N/A

Notes:

Hyde Park Academy High School
6220 South Stony Island Avenue • Chicago, IL 60637
(773) 535-0880 • Fax: (773) 535-0633

Website:	www.cps.k12.il.us	Email:	See website
Principal:	Dr. Sandra Smith	Admissions:	Ms. Ada Lockhart
# in School:	1,800	# Freshmen:	600
Class Size:	17–18	Student/Faculty Ratio:	20:1
Tuition:	N/A	Other Expenditures:	N/A

Profile:
Region 5. Magnet school. College prep. IB program.* Listed in *U.S. News and World Report's* "96 Oustanding American High Schools," January, 1999.

Public Transportation:
CTA el: Cottage Grove Boulevard.

Dress Code:
Appropriate casual, jeans acceptable.

Admission Requirements:
Priority given to students who reside in Region 5. *Separate application required.

Scholarships:
N/A

Notes:

Public High Schools • Coed

Jones Academic Magnet College Preparatory High School
606 South State Street • Chicago, IL 60605
(773) 534-8600 • Fax: (773) 534-8625

Website:	www.cps.k12.il.us	Email:	See website
Principal:	Dr. Cynthia Barror	Admissions:	Ms. Maureen Lai
# in School:	700	# Freshmen:	150
Class Size:	28	Student/Faculty Ratio:	21:1
Tuition:	N/A	Other Expenditures:	N/A

Profile:
Region 3. Magnet school. College prep. Rigorous academic program; all honors and AP courses. Selective Enrollment School. Academy of Finance. Options for Knowledge Program. ETC Program: information technology, music, theater, visual art. College and Business Partnership Programs. Principal awarded Outstanding Leadership Award by the Chicago Principal and Administrators Association.

Public Transportation:
CTA el: Red or Blue Lines.

Dress Code:
Appropriate casual, jeans acceptable.

Admission Requirements:
Selective Enrollment Application, minimum stanine of five in math and reading on 7th grade standardized exams.

Scholarships:
N/A

Notes:

Public High Schools • Coed

Benito Juarez Community Academy
2150 South Laflin Street • Chicago, IL 60608
(773) 534-7030 • Fax: (773) 534-7058

Website:	www.cps.k12.il.us	Email:	See website
Principal:	Mr. Natividad Loredo	Admissions:	Ms. Christy Hoffman
# in School:	1,500	# Freshmen:	500
Class Size:	30	Student/Faculty Ratio:	20:1
Tuition:	N/A	Other Expenditures:	N/A

Profile:
Region 3. Magnet school. College and career prep. Serving the Pilsen Community. School within a school. JROTC Program (Marines). Math, Science, and Technology Academy.* ETC Program: JROTC, Police and Firefighter Academy, CISCO, nursing. Daily 90-minute English instruction.

Public Transportation:
CTA bus: Ashland Avenue.

Dress Code:
Black slacks or skirt, white top.

Admission Requirements:
*Priority is given to students who reside in Region 3.

Scholarships:
N/A

Notes:

The Report Card

Public High Schools • Coed

Percy L. Julian High School
10330 South Elizabeth Street • Chicago, IL 60643
(773) 535-5170 • Fax: (773) 535-5178

Website:	www.cps.k12.il.us	Email:	See website
Principal:	Mr. William Harris	Admissions:	Ms. Bernadelle Cyrus
# in School:	2,000	# Freshmen:	600
Class Size:	30	Student/Faculty Ratio:	20:1
Tuition:	N/A	Other Expenditures:	N/A

Profile:
Region 6. Magnet school. College prep. with special emphasis on math, science and computer technology. AP courses. Medical Career Academy.* Career Pathways: information technology, computer maintenance, carpentry, culinary arts, fashion design, medical, health and radio/TV.

Public Transportation:
CTA bus: Vincennes Avenue, 103rd Streets.

Dress Code:
Appropriate casual, jeans acceptable.

Admission Requirements:
Students must reside in Region 6. *Standardized test scores at/or above grade level, principal recommendation, C+ or higher average.

Scholarships:
N/A

Notes:

Public High Schools • Co-ed

Thomas Kelly High School
4136 South California Avenue • Chicago, IL 60632
(773) 535-4900 • Fax: (773) 535-4841

Website:	www.cps.k12.il.us	Email:	See website
Principal:	Mr. Al Pretkelis	Admissions:	Ms. Veronica Castilleja
# in School:	2,300	# Freshmen:	1,000
Class Size:	28	Student/Faculty Ratio:	2:1
Tuition:	N/A	Other Expenditures:	N/A

Profile:
Region 4. Magnet school: fine and performing arts magnet programs (band, chorus, studio art). College and career prep. IB program.* Metropolitan Studies. International Language Academy: Spanish, Chinese. Career Academy: drafting, CISCO Computer Networking, radio/TV, computer-aided drafting.

Public Transportation:
CTA bus: Archer, California Avenues.

Dress Code:
Appropriate casual, jeans acceptable.

Admission Requirements:
Priority given to students who reside in Region 4. *Separate application required.

Scholarships:
N/A

Notes:

The Report Card

Public High Schools • Coed

Kelvyn Park High School
4343 West Wrightwood Avenue • Chicago, IL 60639
(773) 534-4200 • Fax: (773) 534-4507

Website:	www.cps.k12.il.us	Email:	See website
Principal:	Dr. Diana Hernandez-Acoitia	Admissions:	Ms. Gertrude Coleman
# in School:	2,000	# Freshmen:	550
Class Size:	28	Student/Faculty Ratio:	18:1
Tuition:	N/A	Other Expenditures:	N/A

Profile:
Region 2. Career prep. Education to Career programs.

Public Transportation:
CTA bus: Fullerton, Kostner.

Dress Code:
Blue slacks or skirt, white top.

Admission Requirements:
Students must reside in Region 2.

Scholarships:
N/A

Notes:

Public High Schools • Coed

Kennedy High School
6325 West 56th Street • Chicago, IL 60638
(773) 535-2325 • Fax: (773) 535-2485

Website:	www.cps.k12.il.us	Email:	See website
Principal:	Dr. Fanchion Blumenberg	Admissions:	Mr. Paul Lyons
# in School:	1,600	# Freshmen:	400
Class Size:	28	Student/Faculty Ratio:	15:1
Tuition:	N/A	Other Expenditures:	N/A

Profile:
Region 5. Magnet school. Technology Academy. Options for Knowledge Program.*

Public Transportation:
CTA bus: Narragansett, 63rd Streets.

Dress Code:
Navy blue slacks or skirt, white top.

Admission Requirements:
Students must reside in Region 5. *Application; lottery selection.

Scholarships:
N/A

Notes:

Public High Schools • Coed

Kenwood Academy High School
5015 South Blackstone Avenue • Chicago, IL 60615
(773) 535-1350 • Fax: (773) 535-1408

Website:	www.cps.k12.il.us	Email:	See website
Principal:	Ms. Careta Taylor	Admissions:	Ms. Alice Phillips
# in School:	1,900	# Freshmen:	450
Class Size:	28	Student/Faculty Ratio:	21:1
Tuition:	N/A	Other Expenditures:	N/A

Profile:
Region 4. Magnet school. International Language Academy: Spanish, French, Japanese, German. Career Academy: international business. *Options for Knowledge Program. Listed in *U.S. News and World Report's* "96 Oustanding American High Schools," January, 1999.

Public Transportation:
Metra train: 51st Street; CTA bus: 47th, 51st Streets.

Dress Code:
Appropriate casual, jeans acceptable.

Admission Requirements:
Students must reside in Region 4. *Application required; lottery selection.

Scholarships:
N/A

Notes:

Dr. Martin Luther King High School
4445 South Drexel Boulevard • Chicago, IL 60653
(773) 535-1180 • Fax: (773) 535-1658

Website:	www.cps.k12.il.us	Email:	See website
Principal:	Ms. Linda H. Coles	Admissions:	Ms. Marguerite Mariama
	Dr. Pamela Dyson		
# in School:	200	# Freshmen:	200
Class Size:	N/A	Student/Faculty Ratio:	10:1
Tuition:	N/A	Other Expenditures:	N/A

Profile:
Region 4. Magnet school. College prep. Selective Enrollment School. Re-opened in September, 2002. Rigorous academic program. Programs in architecture, information technology, performing arts. Distance Learning Lab. State-of-the-art facility. College Partnership programs.

Public Transportation:
CTA bus: Cottage Grove Boulevard.

Dress Code:
Appropriate casual, jeans acceptable.

Admission Requirements:
Selective Enrollment Application, minimum stanine of five in math and reading on 7th grade standardized exams. Preference given to students who reside in Region 4.

Scholarships:
N/A

Notes:

Public High Schools • Coed

Lake View High School
4015 North Ashland Avenue • Chicago, IL 60613
(773) 534-5440 • Fax: (773) 534-5585

Website:	www.cps.k12.il.us	**Email:**	See website
Principal:	Mr. Scott Feaman	**Admissions:**	Ms. Jo Lipson
# in School:	1,000	**# Freshmen:**	400
Class Size:	25	**Student/Faculty Ratio:**	16:1
Tuition:	N/A	**Other Expenditures:**	N/A

Profile:
Region 1. Magnet school. Serving Chicago's northwest side. Math, Science, and Technology Academy.* International Language Academy: Spanish, French. Career Academy: international business, travel and tourism.

Public Transportation:
CTA el: Brown Line; bus: Ashland Avenue, Irving Park Road.

Dress Code:
Appropriate casual, jeans acceptable.

Admission Requirements:
Priority given to students who reside in Region1. * Separate application required.

Scholarships:
N/A

Notes:

The Report Card

Public High Schools • Coed

Lane Technical College Preparatory High School
2501 West Addison Street • Chicago, IL 60618
(773) 534-5400 • Fax: (773) 534-5544

Website:	www.cps.k12.il.us	Email:	See website
Principal:	Mr. Keith Foley	Admissions:	Mr. Dan Lanno
# in School:	4,200	# Freshmen:	1,100
Class Size:	28	Student/Faculty Ratio:	28:1
Tuition:	N/A	Other Expenditures:	N/A

Profile:
Region 1. Magnet school. College prep. Specializing in fine arts and technology. Honors and AP courses. Selective Enrollment School.

Public Transportation:
CTA bus: Western, Addison Avenues.

Dress Code:
Appropriate casual, no jeans.

Admission Requirements:
Selective Enrollment Application, minimum stanine of five in math and reading on 7th grade standardized exams.

Scholarships:
N/A

Notes:

The Report Card

Public High Schools • Coed

Lincoln Park High School
2001 North Orchard Street • Chicago, IL 60614
(773) 534-8130 • Fax: (773) 534-8218

Website:	www.cps.k12.il.us	Email:	See website
Principal:	Mr. Nathaniel Mason	Admissions:	Ms. Jane Campbell
# in School:	1,850	# Freshmen:	550
Class Size:	28	Student/Faculty Ratio:	21:1
Tuition:	N/A	Other Expenditures:	N/A

Profile:
Region 2. Magnet school: fine and performing arts magnet programs (drama, instrumental, vocal)* College prep. IB program ranked #11 in the world.** Top1 percent ranking in the U.S. for students taking AP exams. More National Merit Semi-finalists than all other Chicago Public Schools combined for the past six years.

Public Transportation:
CTA el: Brown Line; bus: Armitage, Clark Streets; Lincoln, Halsted, Michigan Avenues.

Dress Code:
Appropriate casual, no jeans.

Admission Requirements:
*Audition required. **Separate application required. Students who reside outside of Region 2 must score in the 90th percentile or higher on their most recent standardized test in order to be considered for the admissions exam.

Scholarships:
N/A

Notes:

Public High Schools • Coed

Lindblom College Preparatory High School
6130 South Wolcott Avenue • Chicago, IL 60636
(773) 535-9300 • Fax: (773) 535-9314

Website:	www.cps.k12.il.us	**Email:**	See website
Principal:	Mr. Fulton Nolan	**Admissions:**	Ms. Karen Rose
# in School:	600	**# Freshmen:**	125
Class Size:	24–28	**Student/Faculty Ratio:**	
Tuition:	N/A	**Other Expenditures:**	N/A

Profile:
Region 5. Magnet school. Honors and AP courses. Selective Enrollment School. Mostly African-American student population. CPS Scholars Program. ETC Program: architecture, engineering, JROTC, . Ranked among the top 15 percent of all Chicago Public Schools. Recent major renovation.

Public Transportation:
CTA bus: 63rd Street.

Dress Code:
Beige or black slacks or skirt; yellow, maroon or white top.

Admission Requirements:
Selective Enrollment Application, minimum stanine of five in math and reading on 7th grade standardized exams. Preference given to students who reside in Region 5.

Scholarships:
N/A

Notes:

Public High Schools • Coed

Manley Career Academy
2935 West Polk Street • Chicago, IL 60612
(773) 534-6900 • Fax: (773) 534-6924

Website:	www.cps.k12.il.us	Email:	See website
Principal:	Dr. Katherine Flanagan	Admissions:	Ms. Grace Wright
# in School:	600	# Freshmen:	300
Class Size:	28	Student/Faculty Ratio:	17:1
Tuition:	N/A	Other Expenditures:	N/A

Profile:
Region 3. Career Academy: business/finance, communications, construction, health, hospitality, graphic design, medical arts.

Public Transportation:
CTA bus: California, Roosevelt, Harrison Streets.

Dress Code:
Black or navy slacks or skirt, school shirt.

Admission Requirements:
Students must reside in Region 3.

Scholarships:
N/A

Notes:

Public High Schools • Coed

Marshall Metropolitan High School
3250 West Adams Street • Chicago, IL 60624
(773) 534-6455 • Fax: (773) 534-6409

Website:	www.cps.k12.il.us	Email:	See website
Principal:	Mr. Donald Pittman	Admissions:	Ms. Jan Smithers
# in School:	2,000	# Freshmen:	350–400
Class Size:	28	Student/Faculty Ratio:	21:1
Tuition:	N/A	Other Expenditures:	N/A

Profile:
Region 3. Magnet school. Academy of Finance.

Public Transportation:
CTA bus: Jackson Avenue.

Dress Code:
Appropriate casual, jeans acceptable.

Admission Requirements:
Students must reside in Region 3.

Scholarships:
N/A

Notes:

Public High Schools • Coed

Mather High School
5835 North Lincoln Avenue • Chicago, IL 60659
(773) 534-2350 • Fax: (773) 534-2424

Website:	www.cps.k12.il.us	Email:	See website
Principal:	Mr. John Butterfield	Admissions:	Ms. Marie Simmons
# in School:	1,900	# Freshmen:	500
Class Size:	28	Student/Faculty Ratio:	17:1
Tuition:	N/A	Other Expenditures:	N/A

Profile:
Region 1. Magnet school. College and career prep. Serving a multi-lingual, multi-cultural community. Law and Public Safety Academy. Options for Knowledge Program.* CPS Scholars Program. Bilingual program received "model program status."

Public Transportation:
CTA bus: Peterson, Lincoln Avenues.

Dress Code:
Appropriate casual, jeans acceptable.

Admission Requirements:
Students must reside in Region 1. * Application; lottery selection.

Scholarships:
N/A

Notes:

Morgan Park High School

1744 West Pryor Avenue • Chicago, IL 60643
(773) 535-2550 • Fax: (773) 535-2706

Website:	www.cps.k12.il.us	Email:	See website
Principal:	Mr. Charles Alexander	Admissions:	Ms. Carol Conway
# in School:	2,000	# Freshmen:	450
Class Size:	28	Student/Faculty Ratio:	18:1
Tuition:	N/A	Other Expenditures:	N/A

Profile:
Region 6. Magnet school: world language and international studies. College prep. Serving the Morgan Park, Beverly, and Greenwood Communities. IB program.* International Language Academy: French, German. Career Academy: engineering, architectural drafting.

Public Transportation:
CTA bus: 111th Street, Vincennes Avenue.

Dress Code:
Appropriate casual, jeans acceptable.

Admission Requirements:
Students must reside in Region 6. *Separate application required.

Scholarships:
N/A

Notes:

Public High Schools • Coed

Noble Street Charter High School
1012 North Noble Street • Chicago, IL 60622
(773) 862-1449 • Fax: (773) 278-0421

Website:	www.cps.k12.il.us	Email:	See website
Principal:	Mr. Michael Milkie	Admissions:	Contact the School Office
# in School:	300	# Freshmen:	150
Class Size:	20–25	Student/Faculty Ratio:	19:1
Tuition:	N/A	Other Expenditures:	N/A

Profile:
Region 2. College prep. Serving the West Town neighborhood. Charter school. School within a school. New building connected to Northwestern University.

Public Transportation:
CTA el: Blue line.

Dress Code:
Khaki slacks, school shirt.

Admission Requirements:
Accepts students citywide. Application, essay; lottery selection.

Scholarships:
N/A

Notes:

Public High Schools • Coed

North Lawndale College Preparatory Charter High School
1616 South Spaulding Avenue • Chicago, IL 60623
(773) 542-1490 • Fax: (773) 542-1492

Website:	www.cps.k12.il.us	E mail:	See website
Principal:	Mr. Chris Kelly	Admissions:	Ms. Yvette Vessel
	(Dean of Operations)		
# in School:	350	# Freshmen:	85
Class Size:	17–23	Student/Faculty Ratio:	21:1
Tuition:	N/A	Other Expenditures:	N/A

Profile:
Region 3. College prep. School within a school. New school serving low income neighborhoods on Chicago's west side (first class graduated June 2002). Strong student support services.

Public Transportation:
CTA bus: 16th Street.

Dress Code:
Khaki slacks, white top.

Admission Requirements:
Accepts students citywide.

Scholarships:
N/A

Notes:

Public High Schools • Coed

Northside College Preparatory High School
5501 North Kedzie Avenue • Chicago, IL 60625
(773) 534-3954 • Fax: (773) 534-3964

Website:	www.northsideprep.org	Email:	rnorman@northsideprep.org
Principal:	Dr. James C. Lalley	Admissions:	Mr. Richard Norman
# in School:	800	# Freshmen:	200
Class Size:	20–28	Student/Faculty Ratio:	21:1
Tuition:	N/A	Other Expenditures:	N/A

Profile:
Region 1. Magnet school. College prep. Rigorous academic program: all classes are at honors and AP levels. College credit courses. Colloquium Program (mandatory). Selective Enrollment School. One of two new Chicago Public School System's Premier High Schools. Opened in 1997 and in 2001, received the impressive distinction of being named the #1 PSAE Public High School in the State.

Public Transportation:
CTA el: Brown Line, Northside shuttle bus available.

Dress Code:
Appropriate casual, jeans acceptable.

Admission Requirements:
Selective Enrollment Application, minimum stanine of five in math and reading on 7th grade standardized exams.

Scholarships: N/A

Notes:

Public High Schools • Coed

Rezin Orr Community Academy High School
730 North Pulaski Avenue • Chicago, IL 60624
(773) 534-6500 • Fax (773) 534-6504

Website:	www.cps.k12.il.us	**Email:**	See website
Principal:	Mr. Leon Hudnall	**Admissions:**	Ms. Jacqueline Robinson
# in School:	1,300	**# Freshmen:**	400–600
Class Size:	28	**Student/Faculty Ratio:**	14:1
Tuition:	N/A	**Other Expenditures:**	N/A

Profile:
Region 4. College and career prep. AP courses. CPS Scholars Program. School within a school. ETC Program: carpentry, computer programming, culinary arts, graphic communications, TV broadcasting, JROTC.

Public Transportation:
CTA bus: Pulaski Avenue.

Dress Code:
Appropriate casual, jeans acceptable.

Admission Requirements:
Students must reside in Region 4.

Scholarships:
N/A

Notes:

Public High Schools • Coed

Walter Payton College Preparatory High School
1034 North Wells Avenue • Chicago, IL 60610
(773) 534-0034 • Fax: (773) 534-0045

Website:	www.cps.k12.il.us	**Email:**	See website
Principal:	Ms. Gail D. Ward	**Admissions:**	Ms. Sandrai Stigler
# in School:	520 currently 800 capacity	**# Freshmen:**	150
Class Size:	15–24	**Student/Faculty Ratio:**	25:1
Tuition:	N/A	**Other Expenditures:**	N/A

Profile:
Region 1. College prep. Magnet school. Rigorous academic program: all classes are at honors and AP levels. Selective Enrollment School. Math, Science and World Language Academies. Partnerships with local universities. Rooftop greenhouse, planetarium, and weather station. One of two new Chicago Public School System's Premier High Schools. Opened in 2000.

Public Transportation:
CTA el: Red Line/Clark Street, Chicago Avenue; bus: Chicago Avenue/LaSalle Street.

Dress Code:
Appropriate casual, no jeans.

Admission Requirements:
Selective Enrollment Application, minimum stanine of five in math and reading on 7th grade standardized exams.

Scholarships:
N/A

Notes:

Public High Schools • Coed

Perspectives Charter High School

1532 S. Michigan Avenue • Chicago, IL 60605
(312) 431-8770 • Fax: (312) 431-8843

Website:	www.cps.k12.il.us	**Email:**	See website
Principal:	Ms. Kim Day	**Admissions:**	Ms. Deborah Pusateri
	Ms. Diana Shulla		
# in School:	150	**# Freshmen:**	25
Class Size:	N/A	**Student/Faculty Ratio:**	22:1
Tuition:	N/A	**Other Expenditures:**	N/A

Profile:
Region 3. Charter school serving the area's high school drop-out population. School within a school. Stresses discipline and life goals. Parent volunteerism required. Mandatory monthly student review with teachers and parents. No internet service or library as yet.

Public Transportation:
CTA el: Green, Orange Line; bus: Hyde Park #1, King Drive #3, Cottage Grove #4.

Dress Code:
Black slacks or skirt, school shirt.

Admission Requirements:
Accepts students citywide. Application; lottery selection.

Scholarships:
N/A

Notes:

The Report Card

Public High Schools • Coed

Phillips Academy
244 East Pershing Road • Chicago, IL 60653
(773) 535-1603 • Fax: (773) 535-1305

Website:	www.cps.k12.il.us	Email:	See website
Principal:	Dr. Sandra Williams (interim)	Admissions:	Mr. Lenton Kirkland
# in School:	700	# Freshmen:	200
Class Size:	20	Student/Faculty Ratio:	10:1
Tuition:	N/A	Other Expenditures:	N/A

Profile:
Region 4. Magnet school. School within a school. JROTC Academy (Air Force).*
Math, Science, and Technology Academy.*

Public Transportation:
CTA bus: King Drive, Michigan Avenue, State Street.

Dress Code:
Navy slacks or skirt, white top.

Admission Requirements:
Priority given to students who reside in Region 4. *Separate application required.

Scholarships:
N/A

Notes:

Prosser Career Academy High School

2148 North Long Avenue • Chicago, IL 60639
(773) 534-3200 • Fax: (773) 534-3382

Website:	www.cps.k12.il.us	Email:	See website
Principal:	Mr. John Jursa	Admissions:	Ms. Pat Forman
# in School:	1,400	# Freshmen:	350
Class Size:	N/A	Student/Faculty Ratio:	20:1
Tuition:	N/A	Other Expenditures:	N/A

Profile:
Region 2. Magnet school. College and career prep. IB program. Honors and AP courses. International Language Academy: Spanish. Career Academy: travel and tourism, business/finance, communications, construction, hospitality, manufacturing, technology, transportation. One of the Chicago Public School's Top Ten High Schools based on test scores, attendance, and graduation rate.

Public Transportation:
CTA bus: Grand, Central Avenues.

Dress Code:
Appropriate casual, jeans acceptable.

Admission Requirements:
Students must reside in Region 2.

Scholarships:
N/A

Notes:

Public High Schools • Coed

Richards Career Academy
5009 South Laflin Street • Chicago, IL 60609
(773) 535-4945 • Fax: (773) 535-4883

Website:	www.cps.k12.il.us	Email:	See website
Principal:	Dr. Joyce Smith	Admissions:	Mr. George Szkapiak
# in School:	500	# Freshmen:	150
Class Size:	20–22	Student/Faculty Ratio:	19:1
Tuition:	N/A	Other Expenditures:	N/A

Profile:
Region 4. Magnet school. Career Academy*: business/finance, health, hospitality.

Public Transportation:
CTA: bus: Ashland Avenue.

Dress Code:
Black slacks or skirt, white top.

Admission Requirements:
Accepts students citywide. *Separate application required.

Scholarships:
N/A

Notes:

Public High Schools • Coed

Paul Robeson High School
6835 South Normal Boulevard • Chicago, IL 60621
(773) 535-3800 • Fax: (773) 535-3620

Website:	www.cps.k12.il.us	**Email:**	See website
Principal:	Mr. James E. Breashears	**Admissions:**	Mr. Tim Coburn
# in School:	1,000	**# Freshmen:**	300
Class Size:	28	**Student/Faculty Ratio:**	18:1
Tuition:	N/A	**Other Expenditures:**	N/A

Profile:
Region 5. Magnet school. Math, Science, and Technology Academy. Technology Academy. International Language Academy: Spanish, German. Career Academy: engineering. Options for Knowledge Program.*

Public Transportation:
CTA bus: Normal Boulevard.

Dress Code:
Blue slacks or skirt, white top.

Admission Requirements:
Students must reside in Region 5. *Application; lottery selection.

Scholarships:
N/A

Notes:

The Report Card

Public High Schools • Coed

Roosevelt High School
3436 West Wilson Avenue • Chicago, IL 60625
(773) 534-5000 • Fax: (773) 535-5044

Website:	www.cps.k12.il.us	Email:	See website
Principal:	Mr. Miguel Trujillo	Admissions:	Mr. Bill Meyer
# in School:	1,700	# Freshmen:	350
Class Size:	25	Student/Faculty Ratio:	17:1
Tuition:	N/A	Other Expenditures:	N/A

Profile:
Region 1. Magnet school. Math, Science, and Technology Academy.

Public Transportation:
CTA el: Brown Line; bus: Wilson, Kimball Avenues.

Dress Code:
Appropriate casual, jeans acceptable.

Admission Requirements:
Accepts students citywide. Priority given to students who reside in Region 1.

Scholarships:
N/A

Notes:

Public High Schools • Coed

Schurz High School
3601 North Milwaukee Avenue • Chicago, IL 60641
(773) 534-3420 • Fax: (773) 534-3573

Website:	www.cps.k12.il.us	Email:	See website
Principal:	Dr. Sharon Bender	Admissions:	Ms. Rosemary Hegener
# in School:	2,500	# Freshmen:	800–1,000
Class Size:	28	Student/Faculty Ratio:	17:1
Tuition:	N/A	Other Expenditures:	N/A

Profile:
Region 1. Magnet school: fine and performing arts programs (band, orchestra, vocal). Academy of Finance.

Public Transportation:
CTA bus: Milwaukee, Addison Avenues.

Dress Code:
Dark blue slacks or skirt, white polo shirt with collar.

Admission Requirements:
Priority given to students who reside in Region 1.

Scholarships:
N/A

Notes:

Public High Schools • Coed

Senn Metropolitan High School
5900 North Glenwood Avenue • Chicago, IL 60660
(773) 534-2365 • Fax: (773) 534-2369

Website:	www.cps.k12.il.us	Email:	See website
Principal:	Ms. Judith Hernandez	Admissions:	Ms. Mary Pat McKenna
# in School:	1,800	# Freshmen:	500 - 600
Class Size:	20–30	Student/Faculty Ratio:	17:1
Tuition:	N/A	Other Expenditures:	N/A

Profile:
Region 1. Magnet school. IB program. Technology Academy. School within a school.

Public Transportation:
CTA bus: Clark Street, Broadway.

Dress Code:
Khaki or dark color slacks, white shirt.

Admission Requirements:
Accepts students citywide.

Scholarships:
N/A

Notes:

Public High Schools • Coed

Simeon Vocational Career Academy

8235 South Vincennes Avenue • Chicago, IL 60620
(773) 535-3200 • Fax: (773) 535-3465

Website:	www.cps.k12.il.us	Email:	See website
Principal:	Mr. John Everett	Admissions:	Ms. V. Hall
# in School:	1,400	# Freshmen:	400
Class Size:	28	Student/Faculty Ratio:	20:1
Tuition:	N/A	Other Expenditures:	N/A

Profile:
Region 5. Magnet school. Career Academy: business/finance, communications, construction, cosmetology, hospitality, manufacturing, performing arts, transportation.

Public Transportation:
CTA bus: Vincennes Avenue.

Dress Code:
Appropriate casual, jeans acceptable.

Admission Requirements:
Accepts students citywide. Transcripts, discipline, tardiness.

Scholarships:
N/A

Notes:

Public High Schools • Coed

South Shore Community Academy

7529 South Constance Avenue • Chicago, IL 60649
(773) 535-6180 • Fax: (773) 535-6079

Website:	www.cps.k12.il.us	Email:	See website
Principal:	Dr. Larry Thomas	Admissions:	Ms. Pam Warner
# in School:	1,000	# Freshmen:	300–500
Class Size:	25	Student/Faculty Ratio:	18:1
Tuition:	N/A	Other Expenditures:	N/A

Profile:
Region 5. Magnet school. Math, Science, and Technology Academy.

Public Transportation:
CTA bus: 75th Street, Stony Island.

Dress Code:
Dark slacks or skirt, blue or green school shirt.

Admission Requirements:
Priority is given to students who reside in Region 5.

Scholarships:
N/A

Notes:

Public High Schools • Coed

Jesse Spaulding High School
1628 West Washington Boulevard • Chicago, IL 60612
(773) 534-7400 • Fax: (773) 534-7394

Website:	www.cps.k12.il.us	Email:	See website
Principal:	Ms. Bertha Buchanan	Admissions:	Ms. Sharon Juntunen
# in School:	500	# Freshmen:	60–100
Class Size:	28	Student/Faculty Ratio:	14:1
Tuition:	N/A	Other Expenditures:	N/A

Profile:
Region 3. Career prep. Vocational education programs.

Public Transportation:
CTA el: Lake Street; bus: Madison/Paulina Streets, Madison Street/Ashland Avenue.

Dress Code:
Appropriate casual, jeans acceptable.

Admission Requirements:
Accepts students citywide.

Scholarships:
N/A

Notes:

The Report Card

Public High Schools • Coed

Steinmetz Academic Centre
3030 North Mobile Avenue • Chicago, IL 60634
(773) 534-3030 • Fax: (773) 534-3151

Website:	www.cps.k12.il.us	Email:	See website
Principal:	Dr. C. Kiamos	Admissions:	Mrs. A.J. Halfar
# in School:	2,400	# Freshmen:	400–500
Class Size:	20–28	Student/Faculty Ratio:	19:1
Tuition:	N/A	Other Expenditures:	N/A

Profile:
Region 2. Magnet school. IB program. Full-site JROTC Academy (Army).* International Language Academy: Spanish, Polish. Career Academy: international business, graphics.

Public Transportation:
CTA bus: Belmont Avenue, Narragansett, Diversey.

Dress Code:
Appropriate casual, jeans acceptable. *Government standard military uniform.

Admission Requirements:
Priority is given to students who reside in Region 2.

Scholarships:
N/A

Notes:

Public High Schools • Coed

Sullivan High School
6631 North Bosworth Avenue • Chicago, IL 60626
(773) 534-2000 • Fax: (773) 534-2141

Website:	www.cps.k12.il.us	Email:	See website
Principal:	Ms. Kathryn Ruffalo	Admissions:	Mr. Craig Hahn
# in School:	1,500	# Freshmen:	300–400
Class Size:	28	Student/Faculty Ratio:	15:1
Tuition:	N/A	Other Expenditures:	N/A

Profile:
Region 1. Magnet school. College and career prep. Paideia Program.* Medical Career Academy.**

Public Transportation:
CTA bus: Clark Street.

Dress Code:
Appropriate, casual, jeans acceptable.

Admission Requirements:
Priority is given to students who reside in Region 1. *Interview required. **Separate application, standardized test scores at or above grade level, principal recommendation, C+ or better average.

Scholarships:
N/A

Notes:

The Report Card

Public High Schools • Coed

William Howard Taft High School
6545 West Hurlbut Street • Chicago, IL 60631
(773) 534-1000 • Fax: (773) 534-1027

Website:	www.cps.k12.il.us	Email:	See website
Principal: Arthur N. Tarvadian, Ph.D.		Admissions:	Ms. Penny Glas
# in School:	1,600	# Freshmen:	800
Class Size:	28	Student/Faculty Ratio:	17:1
Tuition:	N/A	Other Expenditures:	N/A

Profile:
Region 1. Magnet school. College and career prep. Affiliated IB program.* Full-site JROTC Academy (Navy).** CISCO Program. Advanced computer studies.

Public Transportation:
CTA el: Blue Line; bus:#68 Northwest Highway.

Dress Code:
Blue or black slacks or skirt, white shirt with collar. **Government standard military uniform.

Admission Requirements:
Students must reside in Region 1. *Separate application required.

Scholarships:
N/A

Notes:

The Report Card

Public High Schools • Coed

Tilden Community Career Academy
4747 South Union Avenue • Chicago, IL 60609
(773) 535-1625 • Fax: (773) 535-1866

Website:	www.cps.k12.il.us	Email:	See website
Principal:	Ms. Phyllis Hammond	Admissions:	Dr. Michael Jacobson
# in School:	1,000	# Freshmen:	500
Class Size:	28	Student/Faculty Ratio:	20:1
Tuition:	N/A	Other Expenditures:	N/A

Profile:
Region 4. Magnet school. Career prep. Full-site JROTC Academy (Army).* Academy of Finance.** International Language Academy: Spanish, French. Career Academy: international business, travel and tourism, business/finance, construction, hospitality, manufacturing, performing arts, transportation.

Public Transportation:
CTA bus: Halsted Street.

Dress Code:
Black slacks or skirt, white shirt with collar. *Government standard military uniform.

Admission Requirements:
Priority given to students who reside in Region 4. **Separate application required.

Scholarships:
N/A

Notes:

The Report Card

Public High Schools • Coed

Von Steuben Metropolitan Science Center
5039 North Kimball Avenue • Chicago, IL 60625
(773) 534-5100 • Fax: (773) 534-5210

Website:	www.cps.k12.il.us	Email:	See website
Principal:	Dr. Richard Gazda	Admissions:	Ms. Holly Dinkel
# in School:	1,500	# Freshmen:	450
Class Size:	28	Student/Faculty Ratio:	24:1
Tuition:	N/A	Other Expenditures:	N/A

Profile:
Region 1. Magnet school. College prep. Honors and AP courses. Rigorous academic program. Serving Chicago's northwest side. College credit courses. Advanced computer studies, math and science programs. Scholars Program.* Options for Knowledge Program. Listed in *U.S. News and World Report's* "96 Oustanding American High Schools," January, 1999.

Public Transportation:
CTA el: Brown Line; bus: Foster/Kimball Avenues.

Dress Code:
Appropriate casual, jeans acceptable.

Admission Requirements:
Options for Knowledge application. *Scholars application, essay, recommendations; lottery selection.

Scholarships:
N/A

Notes:

The Report Card

Public High Schools • Coed

Washington High School
3535 East 114th Street • Chicago, IL 60617
(773) 535-5725 • Fax: (773) 535-5038

Website:	www.cps.k12.il.us	Email:	See website
Principal:	Ms. Wanda Rivera-Vidal	Admissions:	Ms. Linda Harston
# in School:	1,500	# Freshmen:	500
Class Size:	28	Student/Faculty Ratio:	18:1
Tuition:	N/A	Other Expenditures:	N/A

Profile:
Region 6. Magnet school. College and career prep. Serving Chicago's southeast side. IB program. International Language Academy: Spanish. Career Academy: international business. Options for Knowledge Program.

Public Transportation:
CTA bus: 114th Street.

Dress Code:
Appropriate casual, jeans acceptable.

Admission Requirements:
Options for Knowledge application; lottery selection.

Scholarships:
N/A

Notes:

The Report Card

Public High Schools • Coed

Wells Community Academy High School
936 North Ashland Avenue • Chicago, IL 60622
(773) 534-7010 • Fax: (773) 534-7078

Website:	www.cps.k12.il.us	Email:	See website
Principal:	Ms. Carmen Martinez	Admissions:	Ms. Alma Delgado
# in School:	1,200	# Freshmen:	200–300
Class Size:	28	Student/Faculty Ratio:	15:1
Tuition:	N/A	Other Expenditures:	N/A

Profile:
Region 2. Magnet school. College and career prep. Serving Chicago's West Town community. Honors and AP courses. Technology Academy. Law and Public Safety Academy.

Public Transportation:
CTA bus: Ashland Avenue.

Dress Code:
Black slacks or skirt, white top.

Admission Requirements:
Students must reside in Region 2. If space allows, Options for Knowledge application required for student residing outside Region 2; lottery selection.

Scholarships:
N/A

Notes:

Public High Schools • Coed

Westinghouse Career Academy
3301 West Franklin Boulevard • Chicago, IL 60624
(773) 534-6400 • Fax: (773) 534-6422

Website:	www.cps.k12.il.us	Email:	See website
Principal:	Dr. Lona Bibbs	Admissions:	Ms. Pamela Dozier
# in School:	1,400	# Freshmen:	500
Class Size:	28	Student/Faculty Ratio:	23:1
Tuition:	N/A	Other Expenditures:	N/A

Profile:
Region 2. Magnet school. Career prep. Career Academy: barbering, business/finance, communications, cosmetology, construction, health, hospitality, transportation.

Public Transportation:
CTA el: Lake Street; bus: Kedzie.

Dress Code:
Appropriate casual, jeans acceptable.

Admission Requirements:
Accepts students citywide. Separate application required.

Scholarships:
N/A

Notes:

The Report Card

Public High Schools • Girls

Young Women's Leadership Charter High School
3401 South State Street • Chicago, IL 60616
(312) 949-9400 • Fax: (312) 949-9142

Website:	www.cps.k12.il.us	Email:	See website
Principal:	Ms. Mary Ann Pitcher	Admissions:	Ms. Felicia Ellington
	Ms. Margaret Small		
# in School:	300		# Freshmen: 75
Class Size:	Varies	Student/Faculty Ratio:	24:1
Tuition:	N/A	Other Expenditures:	N/A

Profile:
Region 4. Charter school. School within a school. Math, Science, and Technology Academy. Opened in 2000 on IIT Campus in Bronzeville neighborhood. Modeled after East Harlem, NY school. Excellence in education for low income, minority students. Professional Chicago women mentor students one-on-one for four years. The only girl's public high school in Chicago (fourth in the nation) and the only charter school of this kind.

Public Transportation:
CTA: Bus – State Street.

Dress Code:
Navy, khaki or black slacks or skirt; powder blue or white top.

Admission Requirements:
Accepts students citywide.

Scholarships:
N/A

Notes:

Whitney M. Young Magnet High School
211 South Laflin Street • Chicago, IL 60607
(773) 534-7500 • Fax: (773) 534-7261

Website:	www.cps.k12.il.us	Email:	See website
Principal:	Ms. Joyce Kenner	Admissions:	Mr. Harold Swan
# in School:	2,200	# Freshmen:	400
Class Size:	28	Student/Faculty Ratio:	20:1
Tuition:	N/A	Other Expenditures:	N/A

Profile:
Region 3. Magnet school. College prep. Selective Enrollment School. In 2001, received the impressive distinction of being named the #2 PSAE Public High School in the State. Listed in *U.S. News and World Report's* "96 Oustanding American High Schools," January, 1999.

Public Transportation:
CTA el: Blue Line; bus: Jackson Boulevard, Madison Street.

Dress Code:
Appropriate casual, jeans acceptable.

Admission Requirements:
Selective Enrollment Application, minimum stanine of five in math and reading on 7th grade standardized exams

Scholarships:
N/A

Notes:

Public High Schools • Coed

Youth Connection Charter High School Headquarters
10 West 35th Street • Chicago, IL 60616
(312) 328-0799 • Fax: (312) 328-0971

Website:	www.cps.k12.il.us	Email:	See website
Principal:	Ms. Sheila Venson (Executive Director)	Admissions:	Contact individual school
# in School:	1,500	# Freshmen:	N/A
Class Size:	Varies	Student/Faculty Ratio:	N/A
Tuition:	N/A	Other Expenditures:	N/A

Profile:
Headquarters for all campuses. Charter school. School within a school. Gives high school drop outs the opportunity to complete high school by attending one of these 25, community-based, alternative schools. Each reflects its community (gang membership, homelessness, early parenthood) and focuses on life skills, self-esteem, and job placement. The only public school of its kind in the country. High success rate for more than 20 years.

Public Transportation:
N/A

Dress Code:
N/A

Admission Requirements:
Must be between 16 and 20 years of age. Contact headquarters for more information on individual schools.

Scholarships:
N/A

Notes:

PUBLIC HIGH SCHOOL REGIONS

Region 1:   Belmont Avenue, North
Region 2:   Kinzie Street, North to Belmont Avenue
Region 3:   Cermak Road, North to Kinzie Street
Region 4:   55th Street, North to Cermak Road
Region 5:   83rd Street, North to 55th Street
Region 6:   South Chicago City Limits, North to 83rd Street

THE ABCs OF HIGH SCHOOL TERMINOLOGY

(C) Catholic schools
(I) Independent schools
(P) Public schools

Academy of Finance (P)
This nationally approved, four-year college preparatory program offers mentoring, workplace experience, and finance-related courses in financial planning, banking, insurance, international finance, and accounting in addition to an academic curriculum. Students may earn up to 12 tuition-free college credit hours and obtain a paid internship between their junior and senior years.

Admission Criteria (C, I, P)
In addition to placement exams, schools also place importance on middle school transcripts, especially 7th and 8th grade (first semester); homework (completed on time); behavior (respect for authority and peers); and attendance (absences, times tardy). Students have actually been rejected by a school because of their constant tardiness. In addition to the above, admission into Chicago public high schools is also determined by attendance areas, racial/ethnic balance, or lottery.

Advanced Placement (AP) Courses (C, I, P)
Advanced placement refers to challenging academic courses that offer college credit. Some schools offer selected seniors the opportunity to attend fee-free classes at local colleges to earn college credits.

Attendance Area/Regions (P)
The Chicago Public School system divides the city of Chicago into six different regions (see page 123). Though no application is necessary to attend a school in the region in which a student lives, three proofs of residency and a photo ID are required.

Blue Ribbon School (C, I, P)
The U.S. Department of Education awards this prestigious designation to only 2 percent of the schools in the country.

Career Academy (P)
Twelve Chicago schools have been designated Career Academies; they offer intensified career programs with an emphasis on acquiring job skills, team building, and entrepreneurship in business/finance, communications, construction, health, hospitality/food service, manufacturing, performing arts, and transportation. Qualified students throughout the city are eligible.

Catholic High Schools (C)
Sponsored either by a particular religious order or by the Archdiocese of Chicago, Catholic high schools offer both a faith-based education in which Catholic doctrine is an integral part of the curriculum, as well as the opportunity for single-gender education.

Charter School (P)
Though funded by and accountable to the Chicago public school system, charter schools operate independently and have their own individual, unique missions. Their school boards usually include representatives from community organizations, universities, foundations, and teaching staff. Charter schools have no entrance criteria and are open to all students.

Chicago Transit Authority (CTA) (C, I, P)
Most high schools within the Chicago area are accessible via public transportation. Discount student CTA passes are available for purchase; students should also carry their student ID card, available through their high school. Call (312) 836-7000 or log on to www.yourcta.com for exact directions to individual schools.

CISCO Program
The CISCO Program trains students to design, install, and maintain computer networks and prepares them to take industry certification exams through hands-on training, work experience, and classroom instruction.

College Preparatory (Prep) (C, I, P)
This is a four-year course of study in preparation for college that includes English, social studies, science, math, world language, fine arts, physical education, and electives for a total of 24–28 credits.

Colloquium Program (P)
Inspired by the Greek teacher, Socrates, these academic programs allow small groups of students to examine a single subject in detail.

Financial Aid (C, I)
At most schools, financial aid seems to be based solely on financial need and is not intended as a loan. All applications are confidential, and parents are encouraged not to be intimidated. A separate application along with a recent 1040 federal tax form is required and, in most cases, is reviewed by an outside agency. Some schools may require that the student provide work study or fund raising volunteer service hours.

Fine and Performing Arts Program (P)
This program, enhanced by interaction with Chicago-area artists and art institutions, allows students to combine an academic curriculum with the study of art, music, dance, or drama.

Grade School Interaction (C, I, P)
During the selection process, it is not unusual for a grade school to interact with a high school on a student's behalf. Likewise, high schools will keep the grade schools abreast of the success of their former students.

High School Fair (C)
A Catholic High School Fair is held in October, usually at St. Scholastica, that showcases the area's north side Catholic schools. For further information, call (773) 764-5715.

High School Fair (I)
The Independent High School Fair is held in October at the Chicago Historical Society, North Avenue at Clark Street. For further information, call (773) 327-3144.

High School Fair (P)
Sponsored by the Chicago Public Schools Office of High School Development, the annual Chicago Public Schools' High School Fair takes place in September at McCormick Place North; admission is free. In 2002 more than 30,000 students and their parents visited booths showcasing all

of the Chicago public high schools and were able to gather information and meet educators and students from these schools. Call (773) 553-2083 for further information.

International Baccalaureate (IB) Program (C, I, P)
The International Baccalaureate (IB) Program was established in Switzerland in the 1960s as a demanding liberal arts curriculum and testing program that exposes students to the humanities and sciences. It leads to an IB Diploma, which is highly respected by top colleges and universities worldwide. Member schools are termed prospective, then affiliated, and finally participating as they move through the application process.

International Baccalaureate (IB) Program (P)
Students may apply for the IB program in their region or at Lincoln Park High School, which accepts students citywide, as long as they meet the requirements (see individual school listings).

Independent High Schools (I)
Many of these schools are members of the National Association of Independent Schools, an organization of 900 schools across the country. Independent schools are privately supported and are not dependent on public or church funds. They must meet certain criteria and maintain high standards as members of regional and national independent agencies.

International Language and Career Academy (P)
This program combines fluency in a foreign language with skills in such fields as international business, hospitality, travel/tourism, culinary arts, and engineering. Students are required to complete four years of a world language and a career-oriented cluster.

JROTC (P)
The Junior Reserve Officers Training Corps is a unique four-year program in which students receive military training within a specific branch of the military as well as an Education to Careers Curriculum either in a school within a school or in a full-site academy.

Law and Public Safety Academy (P)
This program prepares students for careers in law, criminal justice, and corporate security.

Lottery (P)
The Chicago Public School system conducts computerized lotteries to ensure that all students have an equal opportunity for school acceptance. There are three types of lotteries: sibling lotteries are conducted only for students who already have a brother or sister attending the school; proximity lotteries are conducted at magnet schools for students who reside within a 2.5-mile radius of the school; and general lotteries are conducted for all students who are not included in either of the above. Parents and guardians are welcome to observe the conducting of the computerized lotteries.

Magnet School (P)
Magnet schools attract students from throughout the city and offer a rigorous and challenging curriculum centered on a specific theme, such as math, science, fine arts, world language, or humanities. Students must commit to following a four-year sequence of study.

Mathematics, Science, and Technology Academy (P)
This rigorous program offers students state-of-the-art science and technology labs, AP, and college credit courses.

Medical Career Academy (P)
A state-of-the-art program that includes corporate-sponsored workplace experience, summer enrichment, and advanced academics and prepares students for careers in healthcare fields, especially medicine, pharmacy, nursing, health systems management, optometry, and dentistry. Entrance requirements include standardized test scores at or above grade level, principal recommendation, and a C+ or higher average.

Metropolitan Studies (P)
This program incorporates the cultural aspects of Chicago into all areas of its curriculum and expands a student's opportunity with regard to urban resources.

Open House (C, I, P)
Most schools set aside certain days on which families are invited to visit for a full tour of the facility and the opportunity to meet students and faculty. Contact individual schools for their schedule. In the fall, the Archdiocese prints a listing of Catholic school open houses; call (312) 751-5216.

Paideia Program (P)
This demanding science and liberal arts program is based upon the Socratic seminar, which develops cognitive skills. Students are required to take five majors and two minors each year and to enroll in honors courses.

Placement Exam Preparation (C, I, P)
At this point, your student either knows the required material or not, but educators interviewed believed strongly that students who are familiar and comfortable with the exam format will have the edge. Available at area bookstores and libraries, exam preparation and review books give students a brief description of the exam, skill review, and some practice exams with answers and explanations. Educators also noted the importance of taking the time to read directions thoroughly, to read every answer before making a choice, to answer every question, and not to rush.

Placement Exam Procedure (C)
Each year on the second Saturday in January, a three-and-a-half-hour placement exam is given at each of the Catholic high schools. One of three basic tests is given (Terranova, STS Placement, or ACT); their scores are interchangeable. Pre-registration is not necessary, but students are urged to arrive early (call the individual school for details) and bring #2 pencils, a $20 exam fee, and a calculator. It is very important that students test at their first-choice school because some schools (for example, St. Ignatius) will not accept scores from other schools. Admission decisions are mailed in mid-February.

Placement Exam Procedure (I)
Students must pre-register to take the Independent School Entrance Exam (ISEE). Applicants should call (800) 989-3721 to receive an ISEE Student Guide. Students may register by mail, phone, fax, or online.

Choose the most convenient date and testing location (there are test sites all over the country); testing location does not affect school choice. The exam fee is $67, and the test is three hours long. Bring four, sharpened #2 pencils and two black or blue ballpoint pens and plan to arrive 30 minutes prior to the test. Testing dates are from November to February. Admission decisions are mailed on or around March 1.

Placement Exam Procedure (P)
Students first must complete the Selective Enrollment Application (available in late September at any selective school, public elementary school, or the High School Fair) and are asked to choose: up to four school selections; their choice of three test sites (does not affect student's school choice); and dates from December to February when they will *not* be available to take the test (one of the five test dates will be assigned). The application is then turned in to the student's current school, which includes 7th grade achievement exam scores; 7th grade final grades (students must have a minimum stanine of five in both math and reading to qualify); and a principal recommendation and then forwards it on. Once they meet the requirements, students are then mailed a letter assigning them a date and time to take the exam. The deadline for submission of completed applications is mid-January. The exam results are combined with other criteria (transcripts, ethnic/racial background) to produce a ranked list. Admission decisions are made by each individual school and are mailed in mid-February.

Prairie State Achievement Exam (PSAE) (P)
Public schools in the state of Illinois are ranked on the percentage of this exam's results that meet or exceed state standards in grade 11. In 2001 Northside College Preparatory High School became the #1 school in the state, replacing New Trier Township High School in Winnetka, which held the title previously. Whitney Young Magnet High School ranked #2 and Lane Technical High School ranked #18.

Scholar's Program (P)
This academic program offers challenging honors and AP courses. Students must have a stanine of seven or higher in math and a reading level sufficient to qualify and receive dual high school and college credits.

School Within a School (P)
These schools share a building and a principal with either another small school or one large, general student body to create a small-school concept: no more than 500 students, individual support and personal attention, daily advisory, regular parent/student/teacher meetings, and a focus on a central theme.

Selective Enrollment Schools (P)
Student selection is based on rigorous academic criteria, and competition is intense at the eight Selective Enrollment high schools: Gwendolyn Brooks, Jones, Martin Luther King, Lane Technical, Lindblom, Northside, Walter Payton, and Whitney Young.

Shadow Day (C,I,P)
Most high schools offer prospective students the opportunity to attend a typical day of classes with a current student (most often, a recent graduate from their school whom they know) and be their "shadow" for the day to get a feel for the school. Contact the individual school to see whether certain days have been set aside for shadowing or whether an appointment is necessary.

Sports/Extracurricular Activities (C,I,P)
The wide variety of sports, clubs, and organizations that schools offer are an integral part of high school life. Participation is encouraged so that a student will be well rounded, successful, and able to get the most enjoyment out of their high school experience.

Stanine (P)
The Chicago Public School system uses a national standard that ranges numerically from one through nine to denote grade-level achievement based upon mastery of academic material.

Student/Faculty Ratio (C, I, P)
This statistic compares the number of students to the number of teachers, based on the premise that the fewer students per teacher, the better the conditions for learning.

Student Resume
At some point in the admission process, the student will be asked to list sports and social and service activities in which they are involved in their school, church, and community. It is a good idea to keep track of each student's activities and accomplishments for easy reference.

Technology Academy (P)
A program preparing students for occupations in computer operation, programming, information processing, repair, and installation. Designed as a school within a school, the program allows eligible students to earn industry certification upon graduation.

Transcript (C, I ,P)
A transcript is a student's complete academic record of his or her courses of study and grades. School records, including disciplinary issues, attendance, and tardiness, may also be shared. A parent or guardian must sign a release form before the school may release any information.

Tuition (C.I)
Two dollar amounts are listed under Tuition. The first amount reflects the school's tuition for the 2001–2002 school year; the second amount denotes tuition for the 2002–2003 school year. This gives parents a perspective on future costs. Expect yearly increases in a range of 2 percent to 10 percent.

World Language and International Studies Program (P)
This college preparatory program for gifted students emphasizes fluency in a foreign language, development of international communication skills, and study of global issues.

INDEX

A
Academy of Finance, 125
Admission Criteria, 125
Advanced Placement
  Courses, 125
Amundsen High School, 48
Archbishop Quigley Preparatory
  Seminary, 3
Attendance Area, 125
Austin Community Academy, 49

B
Best Practice High School, 50
Blue Ribbon School, 125
Bogan Technical High School, 51
James H. Bowen High School, 52
Gwendolyn Brooks College
  Preparatory Academy, 53
Brother Rice High School, 4

C
Calumet Career Preparatory Academy, 54
Career Academy, 126
Carver Military Academy, 55
Catholic High Schools, 126
Charter School, 126
Chicago Academy for the Arts, 34
Chicago High School for Agricultural
  Sciences, 56
Chicago International Charter High
  School, 57
Chicago Military Academy -
  Bronzeville, 58
Chicago Transit Authority, 126
Chicago Vocational Career Academy, 59
Chicago Waldorf School, 35
Christo Rey High School, 5
CISCO Program, 126

Clemente Community Academy, 60
College Preparatory (Prep.), 126
George Washington Collins High
  School, 61
Colloquium Program, 127
George Henry Corliss High School, 62
Crane Technical Preparatory Common
  School, 63
Marie Sklodowska Curie Metropolitan
  High School, 64

D
De La Salle Institute, 6
Dunbar Vocational Career Academy, 65
DuSable High School, 66

E
Englewood Technical High School, 67

F
Farragut Career Academy, 68
Fenger Academy High School, 69
Fenwick High School, 7
Financial Aid, 127
Fine and Performing Arts Program, 127
Flower Career Academy, 70
Forman High School, 71

G
Gage Park High School, 72
Good Counsel High School, 8
Gordon Tech High School, 9
Grade School Interaction, 127

H
Hales Franciscan High School, 10
Hancock High School, 73
Harlan Community Academy, 74

The Report Card

Harper High School, 75
High School Fair, 127, 128
Hirsch Metropolitan High School, 76
Holy Trinity High School, 11
John Hope College Preparatory High School, 77
Hubbard High School, 78
Hyde Park Academy High School, 79

I
International Baccalaureate (IB) Program, 128
Independent High Schools, 128
International Language and Career Academy, 128

J
Jones Academic Magnet College Preparatory High School, 80
Josephinum High School, 12
JROTC, 128
Benito Juarez Community Academy, 81
Percy L. Julian High School, 82

K
Thomas Kelly High School, 83
Kelvyn Park High School, 84
Kennedy High School, 85
Kenwood Academy High School, 86
Dr. Martin Luther King High School, 87

L
Lake Forest Academy, 36
Lake View High School, 88
Lane Technical College Preparatory High School, 89
Latin School of Chicago, 37
Law and Public Safety Academy, 129
Leo High School, 13
Lincoln Park High School, 90
Lindblom College Preparatory High School, 91

Lottery, 129
Loyola High School, 14
Luther High School South, 38

M
Magnet School, 129
Manley Career Academy, 92
Mathematics, Science and Technology Academy, 129
Maria High School, 15
Marist High School, 16
Marshall Metropolitan High School, 93
Mather High School, 94
Medical Career Academy, 129
Metropolitan Studies, 129
Morgan Park Academy, 39
Morgan Park High School, 95
Mother McAuley Liberal Arts High School, 17
Mount Carmel High School, 18

N
Noble Street Charter High School, 96
North Lawndale College Preparatory Charter High School, 97
North Shore Country Day School, 40
Northside College Preparatory High School, 98
Notre Dame High School, 19
Notre Dame High School (Niles), 20

O
Open House, 130
Rezin Orr Community Academy High School, 99
Our Lady of Tepeyac High School, 21

P
Paideia Program, 130
Francis W. Parker School, 41
Walter Payton College Preparatory High School, 100

Perspectives Charter High School, 101
Phillips Academy, 102
Placement Exam Preparation, 130
Placement Exam Procedure, 130,131
Prairie State Achievement (PSAE) Exam, 131
Prosser Career Academy High School, 103
Public School Regions, 123

R
Regina Dominican High School, 22
Resurrection High School, 23
Richards Career Academy, 104
Paul Robeson High School, 105
Roosevelt High School, 106
Roycemore School, 42

S
Scholar's Program, 131
School within a School, 132
Schurz High School, 107
Selective Enrollment Schools, 132
Senn Metropolitan High School, 108
Shadow Day, 132
Simeon Vocational Career Academy, 109
South Shore Community Academy, 110
Jesse Spaulding High School, 111
Sports/Extracurricular Activities, 132
St. Benedict High School, 24
St. Francis de Sales High School, 25
St. Gregory High School, 26
St. Ignatius College Prep. High School, 27
St. Patrick High School, 28
St. Rita of Cascia High School, 29
St. Scholastica High School, 30
Stanine, 132

Steinmetz Academic Centre, 112
Student/Faculty Ratio, 132
Student Resume, 133
Sullivan High School, 113

T
William Howard Taft High School, 114
Technology Academy, 133
Tilden Community Career Academy, 115
Transcripts, 133
Trinity High School, 31
Tuition, 133

U
The University of Chicago Laboratory Schools, 43

V
Von Steuben Metropolitan Science Center, 116

W
Washington High School, 117
Wells Community Academy High School, 118
Westinghouse Career Academy, 119
Woodlands Academy of the Sacred Heart, 32
World Language and International Studies Program, 133

Y
Young Women's Leadership Charter High School, 120
Whitney M. Young Magnet High School, 121
Youth Connection Charter High School, 122

The Report Card   137

How to order this book

Send your check or money order (payable to Linda Thornton) for $25.70 ($19.95 plus $4.00 shipping & handling plus $1.75 Illinois sales tax) to:
Linda Thornton
3180 North Lake Shore Drive, Suite 13A
Chicago, Illinois 60657

How to use this book as a fundraising tool for your school or organization

Share this valuable information and fundraise at the same time! A great addition to high school fairs, Market Days, book fairs, silent auctions, PTA, women's groups, etc. Your group will receive a profit each time they purchase books and sell them at the regular retail (minimum order required).

How to enhance your fundraising efforts with a guest speaker

Invite Linda Thornton to speak at your school or organization. Have all of your individual questions answered by someone who not only has extensively researched the process but has already experienced it first hand and can provide valuable insights and helpful tips to your group. There is no fee for this service when it accompanies a book order.

How to add a high school to this book

Let us know if there is a Chicago area high school that you think should be included.

For further information, contact
Linda Thornton
3180 North Lake Shore Drive, Suite 13A
Chicago, Illinois 60657
Telephone (773) 477-8803